Harold V. Hall, PhD, ABPP
Editor

Terrorism:
Strategies for Intervention

Terrorism: Strategies for Intervention has been co-published simultaneously as *Journal of Threat Assessment,* Volume 2, Number 3 2003.

Pre-publication
REVIEWS,
COMMENTARIES,
EVALUATIONS . . .

"**A**N UNPRECEDENTED REVIEW OF CRITICAL ELEMENTS in the psychology of terrorism. . . . Well organized, very readable, and of the utmost and timely relevance. AN IMPORTANT AND CONSTRUCTIVE COMMENTARY on world terrorism dynamics."

Joseph G. Poirier, PhD
Clinical Psychologist in Private Practice
Rockville, Maryland

More pre-publication
REVIEWS, COMMENTARIES, EVALUATIONS . . .

"SHOULD BE REQUIRED READING in the mental health and law enforcement fields. The editor has assembled a knowledgeable group of authors to discuss terrorists, the terrorized, and the tools of terrorism, as well as crisis negotiations and ethical concerns. . . . These authors offer significant information that is not only ENLIGHTENING TO MENTAL HEALTH PROFESSIONALS AND LAW ENFORCEMENT OFFICIALS, but that is frequently FASCINATING READING as well."

Lita Linzer Schwartz, PhD, ABPP
Distinguished Professor Emerita,
Pennsylvania State University

"A VERY IMPORTANT BOOK. . . . Offers insight into the patterns of thinking of a terrorist. . . . The reader is offered a thorough analysis of various aspects of terrorism, including the ethical dilemmas of consultants in such cases. RECOMMENDED FOR STUDENTS AND PRACTITIONERS dealing with lethal violence as well as to anyone interested in the factors that underlie violent behavior."

Bozydar L. J. Kaczmarek, DSc, PhD
Professor of Psychology
and Communications and Head,
Department of Developmental
Psychology and Neurolinguistics,
University of Maria Curie Sklodowska,
Lublin, Poland

"Clearly A BOOK FOR OUR TIME. . . . valuable for public and professional consideration. Law enforcement officials faced with increasing public security situations will find rational and empirical bases for analyzing and responding to crises. This book will be AN EXCELLENT TEACHING TEXT FOR GRADUATE AND UNDER-GRADUATE STUDIES IN PSYCHOLOGY AND PUBLIC POLICY and should also be a resource for high school social studies curricula. As a forensic psychologist, I was particularly aware of the use of contextual analysis and complexity based theory and recommendations; as a long time member of the peace community, I was impressed with the emphasis on alternatives to violence without sacrificing practicalities or losing sight of the necessity for appropriate action."

Sandra B. McPherson, PhD
Faculty
(Violence Prevention
and Control Specialization)
The Fielding Graduate Institute

The Haworth Press, Inc.

Terrorism:
Strategies for Intervention

Terrorism: Strategies for Intervention has been co-published simultaneously as *Journal of Threat Assessment*, Volume 2, Number 3 2003.

Indexing, Abstracting & Website/Internet Coverage

This section provides you with a list of major indexing & abstracting services. That is to say, each service began covering this periodical during the year noted in the right column. Most Websites which are listed below have indicated that they will either post, disseminate, compile, archive, cite or alert their own Website users with research-based content from this work. (This list is as current as the copyright date of this publication.)

Abstracting, Website/Indexing Coverage . . . . Year When Coverage Began

- *AIDS Abstracts* **2001**
- *Cambridge Scientific Abstracts <www.csa.com>* **2001**
- *CNPIEC Reference Guide: Chinese National Directory of Foreign Periodicals* **2001**
- *Contemporary Women's Issues* **2001**
- *Criminal Justice Abstracts* **2001**
- *Educational Administration Abstracts (EAA)* **2002**
- *e-psyche, LLC <www.e-psyche.net>* **2001**
- *Family & Society Studies Worldwide <www.nisc.com>* **2001**
- *IBZ International Bibliography of Periodical Literature <www.saur.de>* **2001**
- *Index to Periodical Articles Related to Law* **2001**
- *Injury Prevention Web <www.injurypreventionweb.org>* **2001**
- *Linguistics & Language Behavior Abstracts (LLBA) <www.csa.com>* **2001**

(continued)

Special Bibliographic Notes related to special journal issues (separates) and indexing/abstracting:

- indexing/abstracting services in this list will also cover material in any "separate" that is co-published simultaneously with Haworth's special thematic journal issue or DocuSerial. Indexing/abstracting usually covers material at the article/chapter level.
- monographic co-editions are intended for either non-subscribers or libraries which intend to purchase a second copy for their circulating collections.
- monographic co-editions are reported to all jobbers/wholesalers/approval plans. The source journal is listed as the "series" to assist the prevention of duplicate purchasing in the same manner utilized for books-in-series.
- to facilitate user/access services all indexing/abstracting services are encouraged to utilize the co-indexing entry note indicated at the bottom of the first page of each article/chapter/contribution.
- this is intended to assist a library user of any reference tool (whether print, electronic, online, or CD-ROM) to locate the monographic version if the library has purchased this version but not a subscription to the source journal.
- individual articles/chapters in any Haworth publication are also available through the Haworth Document Delivery Service (HDDS).

Terrorism:
Strategies for Intervention

Harold V. Hall, PhD, ABPP
Editor

Terrorism: Strategies for Intervention has been co-published simultaneously as *Journal of Threat Assessment*, Volume 2, Number 3 2003.

The Haworth Press, Inc.
New York • London • Victoria (AU)
www.HaworthPress.com

Terrorism: Strategies for Intervention has been co-published simultaneously as *Journal of Threat Assessment*™, Volume 2, Number 3 2003.

The Haworth Press, Inc., 10 Alice Street, Binghamton, NY 13904-1580 USA

Cover design by Marylouise Doyle.

Library of Congress Cataloging-in-Publication Data

Terrorism : strategies for intervention / Harold V. Hall, editor.
    p. cm.
    "Co-published simultaneously as Journal of threat assessment, volume 2, number 2 2003."
    Includes bibliographical references and index.
    ISBN 0-7890-2253-2 (hard cover : alk. paper) – ISBN 0-7890-2254-0 (soft cover : alk. paper)
1. Terrorism. 2. Terrorism–Prevention. I. Hall, Harold V. II. Journal of threat assessment.
HV 6431.T45946 2003
363.3'2–dc21   2003010406

Terrorism:
Strategies for Intervention

CONTENTS

ABOUT THE EDITOR

Harold V. Hall, PhD, ABPP, is a forensic neuropsychologist and Director of the Pacific Institute for the Study of Conflict and Aggression, Kamuela, Hawaii. He has previously held several positions with the federal government. As a platoon leader in the United States Army, he served in Vietnam and Okinawa in 1966-68. Dr. Hall has been a consultant to forensic, military, and treatment agencies as well as neuropsychology and clinical psychology facilities, including the FBI, the United States Secret Service, the National Bureau of Prisons, the Tripler Army Medical Center, the Kauai County Substance Abuse Program, the Rehabilitation Hospital of the Pacific, and others. He has taught a wide variety of psychology courses at the graduate and undergraduate levels and has been a field site supervisor for the University of Hawaii, Boston University, and Hawaii Pacific University. Dr. Hall is a National Examiner for the American Board of Professional Psychology. He has been awarded grants in test construction, violence prediction, and criminality by the APA, NIMH, the Forest Institute of Professional Psychology, and the Bishop Trust.

Introduction:
Psychological Study of Terrorism

Harold V. Hall

The attack on America on September 11, 2001 will serve as a benchmark by which terrorism is judged and compared for the foreseeable future, despite its long and horrific history. This volume on terrorism thus is influenced by the current Zeitgeist in this country, yet care was taken to include concepts and data regarding terrorism prior to September 11th in order to achieve a balanced perspective. This introduction is more of a position paper and a call to values and responsibility than an empirical analysis. It is trite but true, nevertheless, that terrorism begins in the minds of individuals and that knowledge exists to understand and reduce this violent phenomenon.

Typically, organizations have defined terrorism in terms of broad classes of violent acts or unlawful behavior which is associated with unacceptable politically-motivated goals. The Federal Bureau of Investigation (FBI; 1991), for example, along with a host of academicians and others, defines terrorism as:

Harold V. Hall, PhD, ABPP, is affiliated with the Pacific Institute for the Study of Conflict and Aggression.

Address correspondence to: Harold V. Hall, PhD, ABPP, Pacific Institute for the Study of Conflict and Aggression, Carter Professional Center, Suite C-21, P.O. Box 819, Kamuela, HI 96743.

[Haworth co-indexing entry note]: "Introduction: Psychological Study of Terrorism." Hall, Harold V. Co-published simultaneously in *Journal of Threat Assessment* (The Haworth Press, Inc.) Vol. 2, No. 3, 2003, pp. 1-8; and: *Terrorism: Strategies for Intervention* (ed: Harold V. Hall) The Haworth Press, Inc., 2003, pp. 1-8. Single or multiple copies of this article are available for a fee from The Haworth Document Delivery Service [1-800-HAWORTH, 9:00 a.m. - 5:00 p.m. (EST). E-mail address: docdelivery@haworthpress.com].

> the unlawful use of force or violence against persons or property to intimidate or coerce a government, the civilian population, or any segment thereof, in furtherance of political or social goals. (p. 1)

The problems with this definition are that, first, it applies to *criminal conduct*, with the FBI, until September 11th, resisting demands by outside sources that it apply to violent, subversive groups as well. The injection of a political motivation, secondly, takes us into the realm of unverifiable internal cognitions and the intent of the possible terrorist. Lastly, the definition excludes events that are inherently terrifying and morally repugnant. In this case we would include ownership and threat of weapons of mass destruction (WMD). All WMD, by their very nature, are inherently indiscriminate, making it impossible to avoid harming noncombatants, and inherently random, with conditions impossible to control once launched into action.

The definition of terrorism, for the purposes of this text, is more limited and is as follows:

> Terrorism is a form of deliberate and systematic violence by non-government organizations towards innocents with intent to instill fear or to otherwise coerce or intimidate the larger victim group of which the innocents are a member. The direct targets of terrorism are not the final targets. The political, religious, and/or other ideologies of perpetrators and victims provide the motive for the attack, as well as the reaction to the violence, and define what is "good" or "bad" terrorism. Most likely, the perpetrators are non-military who are using terrorism to effect some desired end and do not have the means to accomplish their purposes by directly engaging the military forces of a nation.

This volume proposes that terrorism is always maladaptive because the victims were not responsible for the attack and because of the deleterious consequences to all humankind. Nothing justifies terrorism except self-defense. No cause, history of oppression, or even previous violence against the perpetrators, or any other circumstance, justifies terrorism unless the possible perpetrator is directly in the path of harm. It is always illegitimate, always criminal, and always murder when people are killed except in the unique circumstances of avoiding or attempting to evade or escape violence from others.

Terrorism can be effectively addressed by a combination of insuring moral clarity and superior technology and strategies, with the caveat that even superb technology and the soundest strategies can never defeat terrorism by themselves. The literature on violence and aggression has generated psychological and behavioral findings that apply to terrorism, can assist in understanding and intervening in this phenomenon, and point to the traits and characteristics we need to develop and maintain for long-range successful outcomes (see reviews by Hall, 1999; Hoffman, 1998; Silke, 2003; Smith, 1994; Stern, 1999).

As a first principle, it has been repeatedly shown in investigations that violence and the threat of violence preempt other events for attention and action. This is an adaptive, survival-related response. Terrorism as a catastrophic event almost always sets off immediate responses in those affected, given the opportunity for victims to act. Counteraction thus should be avoided before knowledge relative to the terroristic act and perpetrators is understood. After the 1995 Oklahoma City bombing, it was wrongly believed by large segments of our population, for a period of time, that international terrorists were responsible. This finding calls for temperance and self-control on the part of those contemplating action.

Terrorists believe that they will ultimately win, if not directly then indirectly, by undermining the credibility of a government that cannot protect its citizenry. Terrorism is recidivistic violence, as shown by the nature of the long-range objectives by the perpetrators. Under the umbrella of a massive terrorist attack, other violent groups or individuals may perpetrate further horror. The anthrax attacks are the prime example. It matters not that only a few victims were poisoned. Rather, this was the first biochemical attack on American soil that took American lives.

Therefore, the risk of further attacks on the United States is high. Yet victims and potential victims of terrorism must steadfastly persist in the face of danger. Every group who is victimized by terrorists should expect to confront distress and discouragement until the enemy is destroyed, or unless preventive interventions obviate the support for terrorism. Given the persistence and lethality of terrorists, there is no middle ground. It is a truism that the group or nation which wins the last battle wins the war. Fortitude and perseverance are traits we need to cultivate for these interventions to succeed.

The perpetrator group, victim group, and context and interaction constitute the violent event for analysis, study, and action. Because violence is often the result of mutual contributions, the designation of perpetrator group or victim group should be based on careful interactional analysis regarding who was victimized at any specific time and place.

Not only was the United States the victim group on September 11, 2001, it was the first attack on American soil by foreign enemies in over a half century since Pearl Harbor (the previous attack was during the War of 1812). This tends to magnify the surprise and shock to Americans, as well as their desire to seek revenge or to destroy the enemy. We should apply justice in the true sense of the word–that is, to render unto every suspected terrorist his or her just due, without distinction, malice, or hidden motivations.

Post-traumatic Stress Disorder (PTSD), among other disorders, commonly develops in victims after a terrorist attack. Responses differ as to whether one is the victim of a bomb explosion, a hostage with or without torture, or a witness to the incredible sufferings of those who were directly attacked. A strong literature now exists on treating reactions to trauma, with psychologists at the forefront of such interventions.

Terrorist violence involves a temporal series or cycles of discrete stages: planning, executing the violence, the immediate aftermath, and eventual return to typical ways of behaving. Interventions and strategies, all of partial effectiveness, can be linked to any stage in the violence sequence. For example, target hardening is often utilized as a (secondary) preventive strategy but is of limited usefulness, as shown by the successful bombing of the U.S. Marine Corps barracks in Lebanon in 1983. In essence, terrorism cannot be totally eliminated without dealing with the core issues in terrorism and all of the stages of the violence cycle.

Deliberate deception by the perpetrator typically occurs at every stage of the terrorism sequence and is of several types: minimizing, denying, misattribution, and exaggerating strengths and weaknesses. Deception should be taken into account in order to plan intervention effectively. Because of its pervasiveness, there is a critical need for the development of deception analysis and deception-detecting instrumentation. (Imagine deception-detecting software that works with battlefield laptops and gives almost instantaneous feedback on truth telling). Yet we repeat that no technological advance or breakthrough, alone or in combination with other methods, will defeat terrorism. This means that we need to put as much effort into conflict resolution and other peaceful means and avoid a purely military solution. Regarding deception, we must adhere to the truth in order to maintain our own credibility. Victims do deceive as well as perpetrators. We should exercise prudence as we wisely judge on all information which may be contrived by impartial parties as deception and distortion.

History, opportunity, and triggers to violence operating in concert against inhibitions are the principle contributions to violence. Inhibitions acting to reduce the incentive to behave violently should be developed and implemented. The HOT acronym (standing for *H*istory, *O*pportunity, and *T*riggers) should be the basis when judging the risk of an individual or group whose activities may be terrorist-related. Violence is *always* a choice after costs are weighed and nonviolent options are tried or excluded. Opportunity factors such as gaining access to the victims, obtaining weapons, and securing transportation are always considered by the terrorist group. The decision path of terrorist organizations and terrorists that leads to violence and its expected benefits should be articulated before intervening. Successful violence is frequently followed by self-reinforcing thoughts, feelings, and behaviors. Violence then takes on a functional autonomy as well as acts as a trigger to future violence. Once established, it becomes highly resistant to change within an individual or group. Terrorist groups involved in the attack on America may *want* this country to invade other nations, engage in killing of civilians, and other acts of killing, as these acts ultimately further their aim of eventually causing the demise of the victim government, country, or group as a function of loss of credibility and prestige.

Interventions that respond violently to violent events lead to self-generating violent interlocks. Delays by self-perceived victims can be in moments or years. Serbs invoked the association of Croatians with the Nazis in World War II to justify their recent genocide in the former Yugoslavia. Arab terrorist groups often refer to Americans as "Crusaders," harkening back to the Crusades a millennium ago. Violence interlocks are usually broken by unilateral nonviolent action, not by bilateral actions. Occasionally they are broken by multilateral actions or by a pacifier nation or group. This is another reason that war and other military actions must be supplanted by primary and secondary preventive strategies.

Micro-violence and macro-violence are functionally similar and tend to potentiate each other. For example, it has been shown that both war victims and perpetrators with a prior history of violence are prone to more violence. Expect and plan for micro and macro changes affecting each other. By this principle, changes and events in the individual and family can have profound effects on the larger society, and vice versa.

Reframing and redirecting our violent mind sets requiring transcending violence interlocks to cycles of affection and gratitude. Training in altruism and advocacy of others of our perceived adversaries should start in childhood and proceed through the lifetime of each individual. We should practice these values ourselves before we impose them on others. Nonviolent efforts have led to remarkable and durable changes. We see them in the civil rights movement, the trend towards gender equality, the increase of freedom and lifestyle options, and even in the greater life expectancy. We must engage in our counter-terrorism efforts while simultaneously training our youth in non-violence as a first solution to problems.

In all our efforts, the dignity of the individual and the superordinate cultural, religious, or national group in which he or she holds memberships should be maintained. No one religion is superior to another. We are all one family, created by one Almighty Deity and inhabitants of the same small, mutually-interdependent planet.

The United States is in an ideal position to take this moral stance. By doing so we can make our own and others' lives far more meaningful and less subject to despair. Whatever one's religious or spiritual convictions or doubts, we need to practice respect for life for ourselves and others. When we and the people of other nations learn not just through our statements but through our actions that we respect life, the message sent will be one of love and security instead of violence and fear. It is a case of being moral to improve morale in the deepest sense. We must be willing to be kind and generous unilaterally rather than waiting for others to initiate or match our efforts. That is the spirit needed to show ourselves and others that we truly care.

The principles and themes underlying terrorism, a form of group violence, are clearly articulated in our first article entitled "Terrorism as Group Violence" by Claudia Clayton, Bonnie Ballif-Spanvill, Sally H. Barlow, and Rachael Orton, who are all from Brigham Young University in Provo, Utah. Their article illustrates the complexity of terrorism and the need to consider the interplay of biological, psychological, familial, peer group, religious, cultural, historical, economic, and political influences on terrorist behavior. As a useful perspective, they identify constructs and data generated by theories of violence that are relevant to terrorism. Next, profiles of terrorists' motivations are scrutinized, followed by a probing of the specific patterns of thinking salient to their motivations. Finally, ways to frame solutions to terrorism are discussed.

The article "Chemical and Biological Violence: Predictive Patterns in State and Terrorist Behavior" by David Paltin of Orange Psychiatric Associates in Orange, California, is a solid contribution to the literature and should be considered mandatory reading by any serious evaluator of chemical and biological weapons (CW/BW). The article uses the Lethal Violence Sequence (Hall, 1996) as a means to assist prognostication of CW/BW use by religious and ethnonationalist terrorist groups. Importantly, for purposes of prediction, the following types of data may assist in providing information related to later CW/BW behaviors: (1) Prior acts of violence that have been directed toward random (i.e., general) population, rather than discriminating targets; (2) Prior attacks that have included detailed planning and rehearsal; (3) Group or rogue state has previously used "sophisticated" weaponry or any type of weapon of mass destruction, or, group has had involvement in food or water poisonings; (4) Group or state has been accused of actively seeking to purchase CW/BW materials; (5) Prior attacks that have resulted in mass casualties; (6) Prior attacks that did not include "red letter" warnings; (7) Group or rogue state has engaged in "ethnic purges" or genocidal programs sanctioned by governing body; and (8) Past genocidal killings were followed by official denials or hiding of evidence. Paltin ends his timely piece with a discussion of solutions by the individual, law enforcement, and federal antiterrorist agencies, manufacturer and industry entities, along with a consideration of government and international efforts.

"Negotiating Crises: The Evolution of Hostage/Barricade Crisis Negotiation" by John Call, in independent practice in Oklahoma, examines the multiple ways a crisis incident can be classified, analyzes the results of hostage incident databases, discusses negotiation techniques, and explores the impact of captivity on the victim. Call recommends that national databases be maintained, together with the development of software programs that can assist during a crisis incident. Call's review reveals general characteristics of hostage/barricade situations of potential usefulness to the evaluator; these include that the acts were usually committed by males under the age of 30 who most often acted alone and frequently had a prior criminal record. Offenders were most often afflicted with an underlying psychiatric disorder as well as motivated by a grievance associated with the incident. Firearms were involved in nearly three-quarters of the incidents with most incidents resulting in injury or death to some of the hostages or to the perpetrator (87.5% of cases). The majority of incidents were associated with suicidal intent of the offender with a history of substance abuse or intoxication. Of particular interest, warning signs were present in over 60% of the cases but were usually not recognized or reported. A majority of incidents were negotiated but the negotiations themselves were successful in less than 40% of the cases. SWAT teams were initiated in over two-thirds of the cases with an assault accomplished in almost 40% of the incidents.

The fourth article entitled "Ethical Concerns in Forensic Consultation Regarding National Safety and Security" is by Charles Patrick Ewing, Professor of Law at the State University of New York at Buffalo and a practicing forensic psychologist, and Michael Gelles who works with the United States Naval Criminal Investigation Service. This article provides an excellent overview of the ethical challenges that mental health professionals and behavioral scientists face when they consult on matters of national security and safety. Ewing and Gelles note the challenges faced in three general types of cases: (1) where a consultant provides input that may have serious consequences for the person in question but no direct access to the individual is available; (2) where the consultant has professional contact with the individual being evaluated but external parameters prevent disclosure of the true nature of the evaluation; and (3) where certain aspects of a consultant's role are dictated or controlled by factors outside the consultant's control. Many cases provide challenging ethical concerns and the article by Ewing and Gelles provides very useful guidance for professionals who provide consulting services in cases involving national security.

Thus ends this brief introduction to this special collection that is devoted to the topic of terrorism. It is hoped that the contents of this volume will evoke dialogue and questions that can further our understanding and investigation of this violent, horrific, and persistent phenomenon.

REFERENCES

Federal Bureau of Investigation Terrorist Research and Analytical Center (1991). *Terrorism in the United States*. Washington, DC: U.S. Department of Justice.

Hall, H.V. (1999). Violent groups and institutions in the United States. In H. Hall & L. Whitaker (Eds.), *Collective violence: Effective strategies for assessing and intervening in fatal group and institutional aggression* (pp. 3-80). Boca Raton, FL: CRC Press.

Hall, H.V. (Ed.) (1996). *Lethal violence 2000: A sourcebook on fatal domestic, acquaintance and stranger aggression*. Kamuela, HI: Pacific Institute for the Study of Conflict and Aggression.

Hall, H. & Whitaker, L. (Eds.) (1999). *Collective violence: Effective strategies for assessing and intervening in fatal group and institutional aggression*. Boca Raton, FL: CRC Press.

Hoffman, B. (1998). *Inside terrorism*. New York: Columbia University Press.

Silke, A. (Ed.) (2003). *Terrorists, victims and society: Psychological perspectives on terrorism and its consequences*. Chichester, England: John Wiley & Sons.

Smith, B. (1994). *Terrorism in America*. Albany, NY: State University of New York Press.

Stern, J. (1999). *The ultimate terrorists*. Cambridge, MA: Harvard University Press.

Terrorism as Group Violence

Claudia J. Clayton
Bonnie Ballif-Spanvill
Sally H. Barlow
Rachael Orton

SUMMARY. Terrorism is approached in terms of individuals' motivations in the context of group violence. Biological, social, and psychological factors that contribute to group violence in general are explored, and the psychological, rational choice, and structural explanations of terrorism are addressed. In light of these constructs, three patterns of thinking of individual participants in terrorist groups are posited, and some approaches to solving the terrorism problem are framed. *[Article copies available for a fee from The Haworth Document Delivery Service: 1-800-HAWORTH. E-mail address: <docdelivery@haworthpress.com> Website: <http://www.HaworthPress.com> © 2003 by The Haworth Press, Inc. All rights reserved.]*

Claudia J. Clayton, PhD, is Teaching Assistant Professor, Department of Psychology, Bonnie Ballif-Spanvill, PhD, is Professor, Women's Research Institute and Department of Psychology, Sally H. Barlow, PhD, is Professor, Department of Psychology, and Rachael Orton is a student, all at Brigham Young University.

Address correspondence to: Claudia J. Clayton, PhD, Teaching Assistant Professor, Department of Psychology, Brigham Young University, 1030 SWKT, Provo, UT 84602 (E-mail: Claudia_Clayton@byu.edu).

The authors wish to acknowledge the editorial assistance of Kathryn Chase and Melanie Hunsaker.

This work has been partially supported by the Women's Research Institute, Brigham Young University.

[Haworth co-indexing entry note]: "Terrorism as Group Violence." Clayton, Claudia J. et al. Co-published simultaneously in *Journal of Threat Assessment* (The Haworth Press, Inc.) Vol. 2, No. 3, 2003, pp. 9-40; and: *Terrorism: Strategies for Intervention* (ed: Harold V. Hall) The Haworth Press, Inc., 2003, pp. 9-40. Single or multiple copies of this article are available for a fee from The Haworth Document Delivery Service [1-800-HAWORTH, 9:00 a.m. - 5:00 p.m. (EST). E-mail address: docdelivery@haworthpress.com].

KEYWORDS. Terrorists, terrorism, group violence

Group violence impacts the lives of individuals and communities in virtually all parts of the globe. It has many sources and takes many forms. It is perpetrated by gangs, spectators at sporting events, organized crime, opposing religious, ethnic, racial, and political factions, terrorists, countries at war, and even by governments against their own citizens. Its pervasive destruction of human potential cries out for better understanding and control.

A comprehensive theory of group violence requires information about the interplay of many factors, including biological, psychological, familial, peer group, religious, cultural, historical, economic, and political influences on human behavior. A thorough analysis of the role of each of these factors in group violence is a matter of overwhelming complexity. Yet to examine terrorism as group violence without acknowledging these factors and their contributions to the thinking of individual terrorists in their coordinated violence is naive. Consequently, the purposes of this paper are to: (1) identify constructs and evidence from theories of violence that have bearing on understanding terrorism as group violence carried out by individuals; (2) discuss three types of explanations of terrorism *per se*; (3) discuss three specific patterns of thinking salient to the motivations of individual terrorists participating in violent groups; and (4) discuss some ways to frame solutions to the terrorist problem.

PSYCHOLOGICAL FACTORS IN THEORIES OF VIOLENCE

We present first some biological, social, and psychological constructs important to understanding group violence. This selection is by no means comprehensive, and space constraints allow for only brief descriptions. Nevertheless, even this limited compilation indicates the complexity of interacting factors involved in the psychology of violence (for a more detailed discussion see Clayton, Barlow, & Ballif-Spanvill, 1999).

Biological Constructs

Instinct in the use of violence to obtain resources. Studies across species indicate that violence may have an instinctual component. Just as animals display aggressive behavior to establish and defend feeding and living areas, attack predators, and compete for mating partners (Wilson,

1975), human violence may be seen as a "biologically adaptive mechanism for obtaining material, and/or reproductive resources" (Manson & Wrangham, 1991, p. 369). We do not wish to imply that possible biologically-based propensities toward aggression are as powerful as innate motivations toward prosocial behavior (see Spanish National UNESCO Commission, 1986). Nevertheless, it is important to acknowledge that biological factors may contribute to the context of the development of group violence.

Certain parallels can be drawn between human violence and animal violence, especially violence observed in nonhuman primates. Humans and other primates fight for resources, including territory and food; compete for females; discipline youngsters, sometimes to the point of harm; and display collective aggression, as in lethal male raiding among chimps (Manson & Wrangham, 1991; Goodall et al., 1979; Goodall, 1986; Nishida, Haraiwa-Hasegawa, Hasegawa, & Takahata, 1985) and raiding and other forms of warfare among humans aimed at obtaining resources deemed crucial for sustenance and survival (Otterbein, 1970).

Violence as the most effective means to group survival. The contribution of sociobiological theories to understanding the use of violence is their focus on risk/benefit or cost/benefit analyses. If the adaptive benefit of attacking, measured in terms of species survival, is greater than the risks associated with the attack, violence will be used (Manson & Wrangham, 1991). Researchers have observed that humans often employ tactics such as using maximum numerical force, modern weaponry, or surprise ambush attacks, to create a power imbalance to their benefit (Keegan, 1976; Manson & Wrangham, 1991). Perpetrators of violence apparently choose their objects of aggression according to the extent to which resources important to survival can be seized. For example, Manson and Wrangham (1991) observed that in foraging societies that had access to alienable (attainable) resources, those resources tended to be the objects of aggression, whereas when there were not such accessible resources the conflict tended to be over women reproductive resources.

Violence resulting from in-group/out-group dynamics. Patterson (1991) hypothesized that chimps label "in-group" and "out-group" populations as friends and enemies, and even as "us/non-food" and "them/food, prey." He cited Eibl-Eibesfeldt's model implying that the ability of humans to categorize others of their species as non-human underlies their ability to kill each other without suffering inordinate guilt. Fabick (in press) argues that ingroup-outgroup bias leads to sacrificing innocent lives when the outgroup is perceived as being powerful and unjust.

Social and Psychological Constructs

Psychologists have also attempted to explain human aggression and group violence in terms of psychological and sociological mechanisms. Early experience, exposure to others' behavior, and individual personality and psychological structure, including susceptibility to emotion, appear to contribute to a person's propensity for violence. Group phenomena that can contribute to violent behavior include emotional contagion, identification with the group, ritual processes, and disengagement of self-sanctions.

Social learning of violence. Social learning theory explains violent behavior as the effect of early experience and exposure to violence. For example, Botsis, Plutchick, Kotler, and van Praag (1995) and Prino and Peyrot (1994) examined the impact of early parental loss and exposure to family violence on behavioral problems. In these studies, modeling of violent or negligent behavior by family members correlated with maladjusted behavior, including aggression and withdrawal, in the children. Other studies involving the interaction of modeling and personality traits have found that boys who scored high on measures of aggressive personality traits were more affected by the modeling of violent behavior than those with low trait aggression scores (Celozzi, Kazelskis, & Gutsch, 1981). These findings suggest that personality traits may serve as a modifying variable to the influence of violent models on subsequent violent behavior.

Psychoanalytic views of violence emerging from hatred. Aggression or destructiveness may be seen as a basic instinct operating in reaction to the thwarting of the pleasure-seeking drives. Although Freud's ideas about the workings of the aggressive drives within the inner psyche have not been validated empirically, modern reworkings of Freud's ideas retain their vitality because of their explanatory power. For example, Kernberg (1995) expanded theoretical notions through his work on personality disorders, postulating that aggression centers on hatred, the chronic and stable form of rage which early manifests itself as an infant's attempt to eliminate frustration. He viewed hatred as "the core affect of severe psychopathological conditions" (p. 21).

The role of emotions in violence. An individual's decision to engage in violent behavior is intricately related to his or her state of emotional development, accumulated affective learning, and present emotional state. For example, anger, an emotion that often accompanies violent acts, has a profound effect on an individual's decision to engage in violence because it disorganizes cognitive processes, limits the ability to consider long-term consequences of action, and intensifies behavioral responses to the object of aggression (Masters, Felleman, & Barden, 1981; Meichenbaum & Gilmore, 1984; Tarvis, 1982; Tedeschi & Felson, 1994; White, 1968). Furthermore, individuals engage in violence in anticipation of a reward-ing emotional payoff (Atkinson, 1964; Ballif, 1977). For example, when the identity of an individual or group is assaulted, losing face leads to a feeling of humiliation; by retaliating, the negative identity can be nulli-fied, and humiliation reduced (Vogel & Lazare, 1990).

Scheidlinger (1994) proposed that three processes combine to contrib-ute to teenage violence. Two of these involve emotions. The first comes from the group's temporary emotionalized state where reason, control, and judgment give way to unbridled emotionality, often found in crowd-like conditions. The second is that of emotional contagion, in which emotional behavior is spread from one person to another. Simi-larly, Hatfield, Cacioppo, and Rapson (1993) believe that emotional con-tagion may help us to understand crowds and group behavior including those associated with Adolf Hitler. Sternberg (2002) identifies propa-ganda and other strategies that use stories of hate to actually create hate against specific targets, thereby justifying and instigating violence and terrorism.

Group processes involved in violence. Certain mechanisms of group membership may also contribute to aggressive acts and violence. Mem-bership in a group increases individual anonymity, personal safety and protection, and some power. At the same time, it decreases personal re-sponsibility. A group mechanism to be considered is groupthink, where the "members' striving for unanimity override their motivation to realis-tically appraise alternative courses of action" (Janis, 1982, p. 552). Char-ismatic emotional energies generated in rituals also create social solidarity and the dissemination of normative group patterns (Heise & O'Brien, 1993). The products of these perceptual disturbances are ex-treme behaviors that are uncharacteristic of the individual under normal circumstances (Diener, 1977).

Moral justification in violence. The disengagement of moral reactions of aggressors may serve as a mechanism to distance people from morally-based self-control and to justify their violence. Bandura (1986, 1990) posited three different mechanisms of moral disengagement: (1) moral justification, which involves cognitive reframing to change the concep-tion of abhorrent behavior into action that is acceptable and needed; (2) minimizing, ignoring, or misconstruing the consequences of violent action through the use of euphemistic labeling, advantageous comparisons, and displacement or diffusion of responsibility (Diener, Dineen, Endresen,

Beaman, & Fraser, 1975; Haney, Banks, & Zimbardo, 1973; Milgram, 1974); and (3) dehumanizing attitudes and techniques designed to reduce the status of the victims of harmful behavior also helps justify inappropriate actions towards those *seen* as less human.

The interactions among psychological factors contributing to violence. The concepts described above were selected because of their probable roles in motivating individuals to engage in group violence, including terrorism. Table 1 provides a summary of these psychological factors, grouped according to biological, environmental, developmental, and social phenomena. In combination, these factors play a key role in determining whether any person will participate in violent actions, primarily by creating expectations and feelings critical to the motivation of individuals for group violence.

We now proceed to a discussion of terrorism, addressing incidence, definitions, and some common characteristics and motivations of terrorist organizations that relate to many of the principles discussed above.

TERRORISM

The Impact of Terrorism

Terrorism is of particular interest to governments, law enforcement organizations, and social scientists because of its impact on enormous numbers of people around the globe. Only a small percentage of the world's population has been directly victimized by terrorist acts, but the very fear of such acts has caused great numbers of people to modify their behavior, affecting the world from the level of the individual to national economies to international relations.

According to the U.S. Department of State (1996), the incidence of international terrorism has tended to decrease since 1987 (see Table 2), but the number of terrorist incidents against U.S. targets has increased from 72 in 1996 to 219 in 2001 (U.S. Department of State, 2002). Table 2 lists the total number of international terrorist events, and Table 3 lists those directed against U.S. targets, according to type of attack. The U.S. remained relatively immune to international terrorism within its borders until the attack on the World Trade Center on September 11, 2001. Since then, the U.S. government has scrambled to deal with the issues of predicting and preventing terrorist attacks and disrupting terrorist organizations that threaten U.S. security.

TABLE 1. Processes Involved in Acquiring Patterns of Thought that Lead to Group Violence

Process	Elements
Biological	Humans have biologically-based constitutions capable of violence.
	Innate tendencies for aggressive behavior vary in strength.
	Basic human needs seek survival first.
	Violence will be used if viewed as most effective strategy for ensuring survival.
Environmental	The biologically-based capacity for aggression can be modified by learning and societal influences.
	Personality traits mediate environmental influences.
	People learn how to behave by watching the behavior of others.
	Environmental influences to become violent have more effect on those who already have developed a propensity toward violence.
	Individuals tend to respond to the things they see in ways that are similar to the responses of those they are with.
Developmental	Early experiences may lack certain ingredients or contain too much of others, altering normal emotional development.
	These abnormal emotions influence decisions to engage in violence.
Social	Hatred is a core organizing emotion.
	The emotions of others are contagious.
	Through identification with a group, individuals disengage personal responsibility and self-sanctions.
	Stronger group identity is created through such experiences as rituals and initiations.
	Internal states such as emotions also impact the decision to become violent.
	Cognitive restructuring increases the value of violence and decreases the perceived extent of suffering it is expected to cause.
	Repetitive violence can become ritualized and rhythmically continued.
	Social roles and authoritarian influences are particularly powerful ways for participants to justify aggressive behavior.
	All motivation to engage in violence seeks emotional payout.

TABLE 2. International Terrorist Incidents, 1982-2001

Year	Incidents	Year	Incidents
1982	489	1992	363
1983	487	1993	431
1984	565	1994	322
1985	635	1995	440
1986	612	1996	296
1987	668	1997	304
1988	605	1998	274
1989	375	1999	395
1990	437	2000	426
1991	565	2001	328

Data are from U.S. Department of State (2002).

Meanwhile, domestic terrorism in countries such as Israel, Algeria, India, Sri Lanka, and Pakistan, is becoming at least as serious as international terrorism (U.S. Department of State, 1996). Domestic terrorism is also a serious issue in the United States. The Oklahoma City bombing in 1995 and the anthrax attacks following 9/11 have commanded the most public attention, but if violent acts by special interest extremists (e.g., animal rights activists, anti-abortion activists, and right-wing extremists such as militia groups with racist or anti-government ideologies [Centre for National Security Studies, 1995; Federal Bureau of Investigation, 1995; Hoffman, 1995; Ranstorp, 1996]) are counted, incidents of domestic terrorism number in the thousands over the last decade (Doyle, 2001).

Definition

We have formulated the following definition of terrorism, incorporating elements from those of several authors: Terrorism is a strategy involving the premeditated threat or use of unlawful violence aimed at persons (usually noncombatants) or property. It is intended to instill fear in a wider group than its immediate victims, and the public is especially terrorized when civilians are targeted in unpredictable ways, leading to widespread feelings of personal vulnerability. Terrorism is considered domestic or international depending on the group's origin, base of opera-

TABLE 3. Terrorist Incidents Against U.S. Targets by Type of Event, 1996-2001

Type of Event	Incidents Against U.S. Targets					
	1996	1997	1998	1999	2000	2001
Armed Attack	3	5	5	11	4	1
Arson	7	2	1	6	2	–
Assault	–	–	–	–	–	–
Bombing	55	108	96	–	179	207
Firebombing	1	–	5	12	1	1
Hijacking	–	–	–	3	–	1
Kidnapping/Hostage	6	8	4	21	11	6
Other	–	–	–	5	3	3

Data are from U.S. Department of State (2002).

tions, or activities. Its purpose is political, religious, or ideological, and its goal is to gain exposure and/or coerce a government, an organization, or a segment of society into acting in accordance with the terrorists' objectives (Adams, 1986; Bandura, 1990; Bassiouni, 1987; Cooper, 1974; Doyle, 2001; Pomerantz, 1987; Title 33, United States Code, Section 2656f(d); U.S. Department of State, 1988, 1996).

Explanations of Terrorism

The most prominent explanations of terrorism fall into three categories: psychological, rational choice, and structural (Ross, 1993). Psychological theories address individual and group dynamics in relationship to the formation of terrorist groups and the commission of terrorist acts; rational choice theories explain terrorism in terms of cost/benefit analysis by the participants; and structural theories utilize the view that terrorism is caused by environmental, political, cultural, economic, and social factors in societies. More cohesive models of the causes and warning indicators of terrorism have appeared recently in papers by Post, Ruby, and Shaw (2002a, 2000b) and Sprinzak (1998). Most of the factors in these analyses fall into the psychological, rational choice, and/or structural categories. We should note that elements within these categories often are not mutually exclusive, but rather are intertwined. The central aspects of these three explanations are summarized below.

Psychological explanations. According to Reich (1990), psychological explanations of terrorism have not dealt with the enormous variety and complexity of the issue. He observed, "Even the briefest review of the history of terrorism reveals how varied and complex a phenomenon it is, and therefore how futile it is to attribute simple, global, and general psychological characteristics to all terrorists and all terrorisms" (p. 263). As with group violence in general, single-factor explanations do not suffice to explain the phenomenon. The propensities of individuals interact with group dynamics and external factors. The study of terrorist psychology is still in its infancy. Much of the present information on the subject has been gleaned from interviews and assessments of captured terrorists, terrorist leaders willing to be interviewed in secure and secret locations, and even autobiographies of terrorists (e.g., Begin, 1977; Savinkov, 1931; Yacef, 1962). It is often difficult, if not impossible, to distinguish the person's rationalization of his/her behavior from genuine motivations. Nevertheless, there are several hypotheses and conclusions that run through the literature.

Some types of personal background are overrepresented in terrorists. Post (1990) cites evidence from several extensive studies of terrorists' backgrounds that indicate many of them came from the margins of society and/or were unsuccessful in their personal lives, jobs, and educations. For example, an examination of the life-course of 250 West German terrorists (Jager, Schmidtchen, & Sullwold, as cited by Post, 1990) revealed a high incidence of severe problems in the families of origin. About 25 percent of the leftist terrorists

> had lost one or both parents by the age of fourteen; loss of the father was found to be especially disruptive. Seventy-nine percent reported severe conflict, especially with the parents (33 percent), and they described the father, when present, in hostile terms. One in three had been convicted in juvenile court. [They were] advancement oriented and failure prone [and their careers in terrorism] were the terminal point of a series of abortive adaptation attempts. (p. 28)

These findings generally have been confirmed in studies of members of other terrorist groups, although Miller (cited by Long, 1990) describes the typical terrorist as being a single male from a middle- or upper-class background, relatively well-educated, although often a university drop-out, who was likely to have joined the group while attending a university.

Tedeschi and Felson (1994) emphasize that learning from the repeated success of aggressive behavior is a major factor in encouraging groups to engage in violence. Terrorists capitalize on this fact among themselves by continually associating violence with the achievement of success through brainwashing, modeling, and reinforcement. There can be little doubt that they understand that building certain emotional expectations for success is a critical factor in maintaining organized aggressive behavior. Such learning takes place within terrorist groups as new recruits are gradually indoctrinated in terrorist ideology and behavior (Bandura, 1990).

The literature indicates that terrorists usually are not mentally disturbed, as is commonly believed (Crenshaw, 1981; Heskin, 1980; Long, 1990; Post, 1984). In fact, the recruiting processes used by terrorist groups typically are very selective, as significant psychopathology tends to prove detrimental to group interactions as well as the ability of the group to carry out missions (Hudson, 1999). Although there is no striking psychopathology or particular personality type that can be considered diagnostic, some traits and tendencies do appear to be overrepresented in this population.

Low self-esteem and lack of success in their personal lives seem to be common among members of terrorist groups (Long, 1990; Post, 1990). Long (1990) states that people with low self-esteem:

> tend to place unrealistically high demands on themselves and, when confronted with failure, to raise rather than lower their aspirations. Bitter at failure, they tend to be drawn to groups espousing equally unrealistic aspirations. They commonly feel out of control of their own lives and are convinced that their lives are controlled by external sources. (p. 18)

This may account for the hatred of outside forces which they express by terrorist ideation and acts. Joining a tight group of others who also blame outside causes for their (or the world's) problems and who are willing to express their shared hatred violently may be the first time they feel accepted by others, the first time they truly belong (see Post, 1990). These views are congruent with that of Lawler (1992), who concluded that people become emotionally attached to groups that strengthen their general sense of control. Choices that bring about a high sense of control produce positive emotion, which in turn strengthens attachments to groups responsible for the opportunity to make the choices.

Russell and Miller (1983) evaluated information about captured or known terrorists from a wide variety of sources and concluded that terrorist leaders tend to be more hostile and narcissistic than the average follower. Leaders' images of themselves as the good ideal and of the outside object as completely bad provides "a grandiose self-image that projects confidence and purpose and attracts others to its glow" (Long, 1990, p. 18). Post, Ruby, and Shaw (2002a) found that terrorist leaders with narcissistic, paranoid, sociopathic, and malignant narcissistic personalities who exhibit charismatic and authoritarian leadership styles are most likely to be able to mold their followers into instruments of terrorism.

Several characteristics of a group's ideology and goals predict a progression toward the use of violence, including the belief that it is impossible to accomplish desired changes within the existing structure of the society; a view of violence as a legitimate means of accomplishing change; the group's specification of targets, particularly when this expands from specific targets to larger groups that have some association with those targets; and the ideological demonization of the historical behavior of target groups coupled with the idealization of the terrorist group as righteous, empowered, and justified in dealing with the target group (Post et al., 2002a).

Long (1990) noted that many terrorists have ambivalent feelings about the use of violence that causes human suffering. (Most of his information was gleaned from interviews with captured terrorists, and it is important to note that some of them did appear to have no guilt or moral qualms about their violent acts.) It is likely that hostage taking is a popular tactic in part because the perpetrators can displace responsibility for any violence that occurs, blaming the authorities for refusing to comply with the terrorists' demands (Bandura, 1990; Long, 1990). Bandura (1990) noted that this process also occurs in battered spouse syndrome, in which the batterer blames the victim for whatever trouble ensues after turning him/her over to the justice system.

Terrorists often rationalize and minimize their actions by comparing them with historical events (Bandura, 1990). Such comparisons help eliminate self-sanctions against violence as well as become a vehicle for self-approval serving destructive actions. For example, the present democracies of France, Great Britain, and the U.S. originated in violent rebellion against oppressive governments. This comparison is commonly made during news interviews by members of right-wing separatist groups in the United States.

Terrorists generally are not impulsive, either individually or in groups. On the contrary, successful operations of this nature demand the ability to plan carefully and withhold action until everything is in place (see Crenshaw, 1981). On the other hand, terrorists are prone to taking risks. Crenshaw (1981) distinguishes between two types of risk-takers among terrorists: those who take risks individually, as exemplified in leaders who, as a manifestation of their narcissism, risk danger as a means of self-affirmation; and collective risk-takers, who derive an identity from being group members *per se*, rather than from the group's activities.

A high proportion of terrorists appear to be stimulus seekers. They are attracted to stressful situations and are quickly bored when inactive (Long, 1990). In fact, Zawodny (1978) concluded that the most important factor in the decision-making process of groups that have been forced underground is the psychological climate in the group, rather than the external situation. Inaction is extremely stressful for these stimulus seekers and results in considerable tension if it goes on for very long. Zawodny (1978) goes so far as to say that terrorist groups must actually commit terrorist acts to justify their existence. Leaders sense the buildup of tension and plan terrorist activity in order to release the group's aggressions, rather than risking the possibility that they will turn on themselves (or their leader). Post (1990) asserted that this climate fosters "groupthink," leading to riskier choices than an individual alone would make.

Terrorist leaders use calculated procedures to actively and continually socially "engineer" the emotions of fellow terrorists. Heise and O'Brien (1993) found that emotions that erupt during social interaction in terrorist groups are judged for suitability according to the cultural and ideological standards of the group. These emotions are managed in order to produce culturally acceptable displays that yield social accord in the sense that individuals' constellations of emotional meaning resonate with or suppress each other during social interaction. Thus, norms emerge that reflect the composition of the group.

Terrorists use coercion as a form of social influence. Tedeschi and Felson (1994) have identified three primary social motives for using coercion: (1) to influence others to obtain some benefit; (2) to express grievances and establish justice; and (3) to assert or defend social identities. Although one of these motives may be salient in any given coercive episode, it is not unusual for all three to be implicated in a single episode. According to this model, individuals engage in a limited form of rationality based on their perceptions of benefits and costs and probabilities of success. But decisions are often made quickly, under the influence of emotion or alcohol or drugs, resulting in a failure to consider costs of alternative choices.

Bandura (1990) presented the congruent view that *violent* behavior *develops* through a process of gradual moral disengagement. He cited evidence that:

> terrorist behavior evolves through extensive training in moral disengagement and terrorist prowess, rather than emerging full blown. . . . The disinhibitory training is usually conducted within a communal milieu of intense interpersonal influences insulated from mainstream social life . . . Initially [recruits] are prompted to perform unpleasant acts that they can tolerate without much self-censure. Gradually, through repeated performance and repeated exposure to aggressive modeling by more experienced associates, their discomfort and self-reproof are weakened to ever higher levels of ruthlessness . . . Eventually, acts originally regarded as abhorrent can be performed callously. (p. 186)

Moral disengagement becomes difficult when aggressors develop empathy for their victims. Examples abound of hostages and hostage-takers who develop sympathy and compassion for each other as they become personally acquainted. A particularly compelling example of the shift from moral disengagement to empathy is told by Laura Blumenfeld in *Revenge: A Story of Hope*, in which she describes the effects of her coming to know the family of the terrorist who shot her father (Blumenfeld, 2002).

An unsettling proposition is that some terrorists may come to see terrorism as an end in itself. Post (1990) argued that, although the ostensible cause for terrorist acts is the group's political goal, the terrorism is actually the end itself. That is,

> *The cause is not the cause.* The cause, as codified in the group's ideology, according to this line or reasoning, becomes the rationale for acts the terrorists are driven to commit. Indeed, the central argument of this position is that *individuals become terrorists in order to join terrorist groups and commit acts of terrorism.* (p. 35)

According to Post (1990), an important corollary of this is that if terrorists actually achieved their stated goals or demands, there would be no further need for their existence. Thus, their demands in hostage situations, for example, sometimes are set so high as to be unobtainable.

Rational choice explanations. Crenshaw (1990) discusses terrorism as a logical political strategy, a choice made among alternatives, that results from the collective rationality of the group. She outlines several advantages to analyzing terrorist behavior by trying to understand the quality of their choices. The rational choice approach also allows groups to be compared to some standard of rationality. For example, questions may be asked about a group's grasp of reality, its ability to judge the consequences of its actions, and factors that may diminish or enhance rational action. This approach also suggests questions about the real motives of a group. For example, is hostage-taking intended as a bargaining strategy, or are there other motives?

At the theoretical level, the development of terrorism through history can be outlined in terms of rational choice, revealing:

> similarities in calculation of ends and means. The strategy has changed over time to adapt to new circumstances that offer different possibilities for dissident action–for example, hostage taking. Yet terrorist activity considered in its entirety shows a fundamental unity of purpose and conception. (Crenshaw, 1990, p. 10; see also Crenshaw, 1985)

Another advantage of this approach is that it discourages us from dismissing terrorism as an irrational or inexplicable aberration. Indeed, the belief that terrorism is the only viable option is one way by which group members may overcome their moral compunctions (Bandura, 1990).

The rational choice approach highlights the specific advantages and costs of terrorism. It can help us understand several circumstances under which extremist groups find terrorism useful. For example, terrorism often has been used when other strategies have failed, and its development can be the result of a learning process. Terrorists learn from others' examples as well as from their own experience, and this process is particularly important because of the intense media coverage and instant world-wide communication now available. Sprinzak (1998) posits that a sense of immediacy of a threat and the perception that terrorism is the most effective way to achieve dominance over rival radical groups are among the warning indicators that a group will employ terrorism.

Terrorism can be useful in setting public agendas, and can even serve as a preliminary step to revolution. In this sense, the bombing of the Alfred P. Murrah Federal Building by Timothy McVeigh in 1995 failed (Lewis, 2000). It caused incalculable suffering but failed to provoke a widespread sense of personal apprehension on the part of the American public, nor did it serve to legitimize the views of the terrorists.

A possible cost of terrorism to the terrorist group is that it invites a punitive reaction that could harm the group, and it can result in increased government repression of activities of the general public, which can result in diminished popular support. Also, governments may suppress active dissent of any kind in the name of cracking down on terrorism (Morarji, 2002). The fact that terrorism may foster further government repression may actually be advantageous to the terrorists insofar as it heightens public discontent (Crenshaw, 1990).

An important example of domestic terrorism in America that did not have much impact on the public or governmental perception of terrorism is the biological attacks in Wasco County, Oregon, carried out in 1984 by followers of the Bhagwan Shree Rajneesh (Miller, Engelberg, & Broad, 2001). These incidents received little publicity at the time, but they revealed significant shortcomings in our ability to deal with biological terrorism.

In spite of warning signs, prior to the 1990s it was assumed that terrorists would not use weapons of mass destruction (WMD) because the worldwide condemnation of and retaliation toward such an action would ultimately cause more damage to the movement than it was worth. However, several groups have since emerged, including Hizballah, al Qaeda, and Aum Shinrikyo, whose motives are based on perceived religious imperatives and involve inflicting the greatest possible violence on the enemy. These groups seem to have no fear of public disapproval; nevertheless, they often do not take credit for the attacks they carry out, finding the personal satisfaction of knowing what they have accomplished adequate reward (Hudson, 1999).

Rational choice explanations also address the reasons that terrorist groups sometimes remain weak in the sense that they are unable to attract large numbers of constituents or garner sufficient military power to effect political or societal changes by other means. They may be so extreme that their appeal is limited, and they resort to terrorism to even the odds. Also, groups may not have the resources, or perhaps the temperament, to do the difficult and time-consuming work required to mobilize large-scale support. Contrast, for example, the IRA, a terrorist organization, and its legal counterpart, Sinn Fein (Crenshaw, 1990). These groups may be unable to test their popularity in any straightforward way, so they tend to develop fantasies about positive responses of the general population. According to Crenshaw (1990), such unrealistic expectations are not unusual in radical underground organizations in Western democracies.

According to the rational choice approach, terrorism may be a defensive response to threat or to a downturn in a group's fortunes, as well as a response to an opportunity. For example, the IRA Provisionals (PIRA) utilized terrorism to counter its appearance of weakness, even though this alienated public opinion (McGuire, 1973).

Terrorist leaders may use poor judgment because they tend to want action. However, impatience also can result from an analysis of the situation that indicates an immediate window of opportunity for success, such as an increase in the vulnerability of the regime in power or a significant increase in the power or resources of the terrorist group (e.g., money, weapons, training, information, strategic innovation, etc.). On the other hand, religious terrorists sometimes schedule their attacks according to their theological beliefs or that cause maximum disruption of their enemies' religious holidays or other sacred times. Thus, Timothy McVeigh apparently patterned his attack on the Alfred P. Murrah Federal Building in Oklahoma after *The Turner Diaries* (Pierce, 1978) and based the timing on the second anniversary of the demise of the Branch Davidians in Waco, Texas, which he blamed on the FBI (Ranstorp, 1996). Al Qaeda appears to lay plans, train operatives, and work out logistics months and even years before executing attacks (Bergen, 2001a).

Structural explanations. Ross (1993) has constructed a causal model based on structure. He posits three "permissive" causes–geographical location; type of political system; and level of modernization–and seven "precipitant" causes (listed in order from least to most important): social, cultural, and historical facilitation; organizational split and development; presence of other forms of unrest; support; counterterrorist organization failure; availability of weapons and explosives; and grievances. The permissive causes act as facilitators of the precipitant causes. This view is particularly useful when superimposed on the psychological and rational choice approaches discussed previously.

Ross (1993) suggested that level of modernization is the most important of the permissive factors. He lists six factors of modern societies that encourage terrorism: "better, more sophisticated, vulnerable targets; destructive weapons and technology; mass media; populations with increased literacy; conflicts with traditional ways of life; and networks of transportation" (p. 322). He also stated that modern societies tend to press for democratic governments. Thus, the more modern the society, the greater the number of grievances and the ability to express or act on them.

The seven precipitant causes have a more immediate impact on the development of terrorism. Social, cultural, and historical facilitation are based on shared values, beliefs, and traditions that foster the development of subgroups within the population. These deeply held, shared views and attitudes foster group identity and cohesion (Ross, 1993). The nature of the society's moral strictures concerning the use of violence are particularly important (Sprinzak, 1998). For example, in Kashmir and Nagorno-Karabakh violence has long been part of the political order. Also, current violent conflict around religion, ethnicity, or class (e.g., Sikhs and Hindus, Hutus and Tutsis in Rwanda, and landowners and peasants in El Salvador, respectively), increase the probability of the emergence of terrorist factions, especially if leaders capitalize on historical conflicts (e.g., the Serbian conflict; Israel and Palestine; Post et al., 2002a).

Regarding organizational development or split, Ross (1993) cited evidence that "most terrorist groups come into existence as the result of a split between the moderate and the more extreme wings of an already-existing organization (e.g., political party)" (p. 323, see also Laqueur, 1977, p. 103). He postulated that the more splitting that occurs within terrorist organizations, the greater the likelihood that at least one of the splinter groups will advocate or use terrorism. Crenshaw (1990) mentioned the Red Brigades and Prima Linea, two Italian left-wing groups that became divided over the issue of whether to work clandestinely or to use propaganda and other organizational strategies to work with a larger protest movement. The Red Brigades chose the former and Prima Linea the latter. Ross (1993) also postulated that other forms of political unrest (i.e., strikes, riots, revolution, and demonstrations) within the population will increase the probability that subgroups will identify and act upon grievances. This is consonant with Sprinzak's (1998) view that terrorism may be seen as a means of attaining supremacy in competition between groups, especially if they perceive that their constituencies are shrinking.

Resources in the form of financial, political, or organizational support also increase the risk of terrorism (Sprinzak, 1998). Specific examples of support include "finances, training, intelligence, false documents, donations or sales of weapons and explosives, provisions of sanctuary or safe housing, propaganda campaigns, ideological justification, public opinion, legal services, and a constant supply of recruits" (Ross, 1993, p. 324; see also Long, 1990). Actual operational support increases the risk that a group will use terrorist tactics more than ideological or even financial support (Post et al., 2002a). Such support may come from internal or external sources, the latter opening the way for manipulation by factions outside the organization, such as foreign governments.

Ross (1993) suggested that the greater the availability of weapons and explosives, the greater the incidence of terrorism. According to Avrich

(1984), nineteenth-century anarchists believed the invention of dynamite provided a "great equalizing force, enabling ordinary workmen to stand up against armies, militias, and police, to say nothing of the hired gunmen of the employers" (p. 166). Weapons can be obtained by purchase, theft, gift, or construction. Many weapons and materials for bombs are legally available in the U.S. Timothy McVeigh, for example, was able to buy materials to make the deadly truck bomb that took 168 lives and wounded hundreds of others in Oklahoma City in 1995 (FBI, 1997). The presence of weapons and weapons materials is particularly high in countries that have recently gone through civil strife.

Ross's (1993) last precipitant cause is grievances. Post, Ruby, and Shaw (2002a) noted that instability in the form of political unrest (e.g., a change in the form of government, unpopular governmental policies, and high levels of political corruption), economic hardship (e.g., high unemployment or great disparity in the distribution of wealth), or social issues (e.g., significant refugee or other immigration problems, or differences between minority and majority groups) may precipitate serious grievances that foster a violent approach among disaffected groups. Ross (1993) parsed grievances into seven categories: economic, ethnic, racial, legal, political, religious, and social. These grievances can be directed against "individuals, groups, organizations, classes, races, and ethnicities, both public and private (e.g., the government, businesses, unions, military, police, religious organizations, political parties)" (p. 326). Left unaddressed, serious grievances can result in the formation of social movements or interest groups that can, under the influence of the factors mentioned above, evolve or split into terrorist organizations.

Another structural factor that plays into the risk or terrorism is "key actors affecting the group" (Post et al., 2002, p. 81). These include opponents, constituents and supporters, and competitors. The characteristics of opponents (e.g., regimes, ethnic or religious rivals, other socioeconomic groups, the media, outspoken critics) can "play a significant role in heightening or decreasing the risk that a radical group will resort to terrorism . . . [and] it is the perceived level of threat that is critical" (Post et al., 2002a, p. 81). Constituencies may be large (e.g., the support of Hizballah by Iran and of bin Laden by the Taliban), or small (extremist religious or political groups), or may not exist outside the group itself. Competition between rival groups may lead to an escalation of violence if that is seen as the best means of exerting domination (e.g., Hamas and the Islamic Jihad).

MOTIVATION PROFILES OF TERRORISTS

As pointed out earlier, there are no simple, global, and general psychological characteristics that hold true as descriptors for all terrorists (Reich, 1990). However, we do believe there are some elements of motivational processes that are identifiable in those who engage in group violence, including terrorism. In light of the constructs and explanations presented previously, we propose three patterns of thinking that together motivate individuals to participate in terrorism.

The first pattern of thinking focuses on *individual and collective expectations of beneficial outcomes from engaging in violence*. The most sought-after outcomes are those which bring positive emotional payout. From the discussion of explanations of terrorism, we learn that those who participate in terrorism likely have unfulfilled needs for belonging and/or accomplishment. Individuals who find themselves in circumstances in which they perceive that aggression can be used to both meld them with others and fulfill their needs to succeed may be seduced into terrorist groups. The specific nature of the emotional payout will vary from individual to individual. For some it will be belonging to a tight group of associates who share common goals and ideologies. To others it will be the opportunity to accomplish something (e.g., putting things right; establishing justice) that will be seen favorably by the members of the group and, in some cases, by their God. The emotional payout may also come from the feeling of being in control. Some examples of positive outcomes individuals typically expect from engaging in terrorist violence are shown in Table 4.

The second pattern of thinking focuses on *the individual participant's view of him/herself as not only capable of bringing about the desired result but personally responsible for doing so*. No one attempts to accomplish a goal without believing that there is a chance of success (Atkinson, 1964). People who engage in violence are no exception. They will not participate in violent acts unless they believe that they will be able to bring about the benefits they pursue. In some cases, these individuals have exaggerated views of themselves, even messianic delusions, and they believe they have been given unique abilities to complete their missions. Such individuals not only believe that they can be successful, but they feel it is their personal responsibility to do so. They often feel that they are the only ones who can restore justice or right whatever wrongs they perceive. Table 5 lists some of the thought patterns that cluster around the sense violent people have of themselves, individually and collectively.

TABLE 4. Some Positive Outcomes Expected by Members of Terrorist Groups

An object of hate destroyed.

A blameworthy act punished.

A misdeed put right.

Justice maintained.

Power balanced.

A reputation established.

A desired identity protected.

Negative identities nullified.

Humiliation reduced.

Group position affirmed.

Negative consequences minimized.

Position of power obtained.

The world freed from less desirables.

The greater good brought forth.

When an individual believes that it is possible to bring about personal adulation from those within his or her group as well as make the world a better place by participating in violent acts, it is not surprising that he or she would be willing to do so. Beliefs that he or she has been personally chosen to bring these benefits about and that the group as a whole will be responsible for any problems that may arise enhance the motivation to engage in terrorism.

Both of these patterns of thinking are modeled and reinforced within a tight group of associates. This leads to intense climates often engineered by terrorist leaders to strengthen these patterns of motivation and to leave no room for inaction. Within this atmosphere, terrorists promise belonging and success and issue calls to serve isolated from mainstream social experiences. Furthermore, these organizations often claim to be operating on higher moral laws. Because their lofty ambitions are often unattainable, they may find themselves in a never-ending cycle of planning and carrying out terrorism.

TABLE 5. Thought Patterns Concerning Sense of Self

They see others as idols, enemies, or fools, all in exaggerated ways.

They dehumanize their targets of aggression.

They see themselves as the embodiment of good having to deal with enemies.

They think they are chosen, selected by God to carry out their missions.

Their personal identities merge with the group's identity.

As the group's identity increases, so does the anonymity of the individual.

They believe that responsibility for what they do is not theirs but that of the group.

Self-regulation procedures give way to group regulation processes.

They believe that they will be safe and protected by the group.

The third pattern of thinking is *the view of violence as the most effective way to accomplish sought-after results*. Wanting certain results and believing that one can obtain them are insufficient to cause an individual to join others in violent acts. Potential participants must also believe that violence is the most effective way, and possibly the only way, to obtain the desired benefits. Terrorism is not impulsive behavior. It is systematically planned, and risks are weighed carefully. From the point of view of the terrorist, all other instrumental steps are judged to be less effective than terrorism. Whether the objective is to set a public agenda through intense world-wide media coverage, send a message of warning, increase government repression which may heighten public discontent, or fulfill some other political purpose, terrorism is seen as the most effective means to the desired end and cannot be explained as an irrational or random aberration.

These three patterns of thinking and emotion must all be present to some degree in order for an individual to engage in terrorism. It is, however, important to understand that individuals with similar innate characteristics and environmental inputs still can differ in their motivation profiles, which ultimately lead to choice of behavior. This may account for the fact that not all individuals who have a propensity for violence or have experienced difficult environmental influences, and who find themselves in groups with enormous sophistication in exerting pressure on them to engage in violence, still resist. For the most part, however, we believe that the processes described above create the thought patterns that are critical in motivating individuals to participate in group violence, including terrorism.

SOLUTIONS TO TERRORISM

Solutions to terrorism are desperately needed and overwhelmingly difficult. We believe the most effective solutions ultimately will be those that address the motivations to violence and the processes that lead to those motivations.

Finding and implementing effective solutions to the terrorist threat necessitates a thorough understanding of its causes and the processes by which it develops and operates. Misunderstanding of these issues can lead to futile attitudes and interventions. For example, the inaccurate assumption that terrorists are, on the whole, highly pathological minimizes the importance of political, religious, economic, ethnic, and historical motivations that must be dealt with in a successful intervention (Hudson, 1999; Rasch, 1979).

Monroe and Kreidie (1997) present *perspective* as a critical piece in understanding and dealing with Islamic and other fundamentalists. They argue that the fundamentalist's perspective is that he/she is a symbol of Islam rather than a separate individual, and that Islamic fundamentalists do not always weigh costs and benefits in accordance with the western perspective. Fundamentalist values and beliefs should not be regarded as subject to negotiation, compromise, or even discourse in the western tradition. Rather, fundamentalists operate under a religious continuum of the private and the political.

Islamic fundamentalism has been interpreted from the rational choice perspective as being a reaction to the rapid modernization of the world with its attendant socioeconomic inequalities. Thus, fundamentalists have often been assumed to be religious and political dogmatists, anxious and alienated, who are committed to a spare, ascetic lifestyle, and they are seen as irrational when they do not act in accord with western cost/benefit models (Hudson, 1999).

Empirical evidence does not necessarily support this view. Fundamentalists are not necessarily poor or uneducated (Bergen, 2001). Al Qaeda, for example, is a transnational organization with considerable modern infrastructure and sophisticated training methods. Although its recruits are most often from rural, fundamental religious backgrounds, those in leadership usually come from the middle and upper classes and have university degrees, often in the physical sciences and engineering (Bergen, 2001a, 2001b; Hudson, 1999).

It is important to note that the perspectives of secular terrorist groups incorporate moral and ideological imperatives as compelling as those of religious fundamentalists. It is crucial that western thinkers not make assumptions based on their own perspectives that limit their understanding of these groups.

In addition to a thorough understanding of the terrorist mindset and group dynamics, comprehensive models for the prediction of terrorism must be developed and tested. Post, Ruby, and Shaw (2002a, 2002b) have formulated a promising model that identifies the critical elements in risk analysis for five types of terrorist groups. They systematically employed the knowledge of experts who were asked to submit lists of terrorism risk factors concerning environments, groups, and interactions for each of five types of radical groups. Factor analysis was performed, and a model for risk prediction ultimately emerged with four general categories: (1) historical, cultural, and contextual features; (2) key actors affecting the group; (3) the group/organization; and (4) the immediate situation. These factors are easier to assess than information about the internal functioning of the group, which is difficult and dangerous to obtain.

Nevertheless, there is a compelling case to be made for the necessity of first-hand contact with terrorists in order to understand them (Hoffman, 1995). The major reason for the dearth of psychometric studies in the field has been the lack of access to terrorists, even those who are imprisoned. There would be obvious problems with reliability and generalizability of information gained from such contact, and there is even danger of retaliation if members of the group disapprove of the findings. Nevertheless, face-to-face interviews and assessments will be crucial to complement the views of terrorism being put forth from the outside.

Intervention to prevent the carrying out of terrorist plots and, in the longer term, to prevent or deter the formation of and recruitment to terrorist organizations is perhaps the most difficult aspect of solving the terrorist problem. Intervention strategies must be developed and the will to implement them be generated. Effective strategies will be complex, difficult, expensive, and not always quick to bear fruit. This makes it difficult to garner the necessary public support for preemptive action that may not seem efficient or decisive unless it is overtly military in nature.

Several overarching policy objectives are important (Long, 1990; Terrorism Research Center, 1997):

1. The policy must be global, emphasizing international cooperation. This may necessitate focusing on the criminality of terrorist acts, rather than on the terrorist groups *per se*, thus avoiding value judgments as to the legitimacy of the terrorists' political goals.
2. Interagency cooperation is paramount. Both the components (the operating principles and specific counterterrorist measures) and the process (means of administration) of the policy must be addressed. This involves patient negotiation and consensus-building.
3. The policy must be long-term.
4. The policy must be adaptable to the wide variety of terrorist situations.
5. Governments should talk directly to terrorists, as a rule, because dialogue generally is necessary to peaceful resolution of conflict.
6. Patience, perseverance, and willingness to forego recognition are necessary in those responsible for tracking down and thwarting terrorists. (Such a low-key approach can run counter to American culture.)
7. Restraint is necessary to avoid premature action that may foreclose the obtaining of further intelligence and to prevent overreaction such as inappropriate repression of the populace, which can undermine the legitimacy of the government.

In determining how to eliminate the benefits of terrorist acts it is important to consider what, if any, concessions to terrorists governments should be prepared to make. There is general agreement that government or law enforcement entities should negotiate to resolve specific situations or political issues only if this provides no reward for terroristic actions. Levitt (1988) suggests viewing the response in terms of four principles:

1. Governments should strive for consistency in their categorization and condemnation of terrorist acts.
2. Clarity of policy is important, notwithstanding the fact that it may evolve over the years.
3. Antiterrorism policy must be credible. That is, it must attempt to make the costs of terrorist activity prohibitively high in ways that are reasonably possible to accomplish. It should avoid extravagant claims about eradicating terrorism.
4. Striving for international consensus is paramount. Even unilateral responses should be made within the framework of collective policy.

Levitt (1988) and Hudson (1999) also discuss political measures for dealing with terrorists:

1. Long-term political measures should be designed to resolve the broad political problems that encourage terrorism. In reality, this is impossible to accomplish fully. Even so, it should be recognized that changing laws, altering geographic boundaries, providing education to change destructive traditions, refraining from inflammatory acts, and so forth, can have a long-term effect in reducing the motivation for terrorist acts.

2. Effective counterterrorist strategies may include identification and capture of terrorist leaders, "allowing the group to reassess the policies pursued by its captured leader and possibly move in a less violent direction" (Hudson, 1999, p. 58). This may accompany strategies to split the group along military and political fault lines. Unfortunately, a military response to terrorism in the absence of political and social strategies is likely to promote group cohesion rather than fostering fragmentation.

3. Tactical diplomacy should be used to "encourage, maintain, and increase international cooperation against terrorism and isolate terrorist groups and states supporting them until they are induced to cease [and to] provide and share technical assistance for antiterrorism" (Hudson, 1999, p. 148). Extradition treaties should be expanded and informal working relationships among various professionals fostered. (The latter is often difficult, as "turf" is so important to governmental, military, and police agencies.)

4. Counterterrorist strategies should be tailored carefully to each group. Comprehensive models of terrorists' motivations such as that of Post, Ruby, and Shaw (2002a, 2002b) will be particularly useful in this arena.

5. Public affairs measures include formulating and publicizing a clear, consistent, credible public policy; dealing with the news media by providing "the conceptual simplicity that the reporter requires without resorting to simplistic polemics that ill-serve the decision-makers, the media, and the public alike" (Hudson, 1999, p. 150); maintaining close communication with airlines, businesses, and other private sector entities that may be targets; supplying adequate travel warnings and other advisories; maintaining a sympathetic relationship with victims and their families; and depoliticizing terrorist acts by focusing on the criminal aspects.

It is important to facilitate aggressors seeing themselves as more peaceful and their victims as more human. The news media may contribute to how terrorists see themselves and their victims. Bassiouni (1987) described problems of media coverage of terrorist incidents:

1. The very reporting of violence may encourage others to commit violent acts.
2. Excesses or deficiencies in media coverage "may enhance the climate of intimidation which the terrorist seeks to generate; this would not only further unnecessarily the perpetrators' objectives, but it would also engender pressures for counterproductive governmental repression and cause undesirable social consequences" (Bassiouni, 1987, p. 183).
3. Intense or repeated media coverage may deaden the public's outrage at terrorist acts and increase its tolerance of violence, thus necessitating increased violence to achieve the effect desired by the terrorists. Also, such coverage can render impersonal or abstract the violence and its consequences, thus diminishing the humanity of the victims and terrorists.
4. Media reports may endanger the lives of hostages and otherwise interfere with law enforcement. This is most likely during coverage of events as they are occurring.

On the other hand, Bassiouni (1987) noted that media coverage also can serve as a "safety valve" by publicizing terrorist viewpoints that otherwise would be brought to public attention by violent actions. Also, the media may have access to intelligence unavailable to official organizations, and they sometimes can serve to secure the release of hostages, such as by agreeing to publish the terrorists' rhetoric.

Patient negotiation with captors may help them come to see their hostages as more human as they come to know them, and as they see the hostages' human value to the negotiators, thus increasing the chances of hostage survival. Also, a patient approach on the part of police or military may help the terrorists see their way to accomplishing at least some of their objectives using alternatives to violence. Unfortunately, highly ideological terrorists are likely to degrade and torment their hostages, who in turn are less likely to develop any sympathy with their captors; thus, personalization often does not develop on either side (Bandura, 1990).

In addition to specific responses to terrorism, intervention in the processes that lead to participation in group violence (see Table 1) can facilitate prevention in the long run. This is difficult, to say the least, but there has been a groundswell of awareness in the U.S. in recent years in response to the many forms of violence prevalent in our society. Awareness of the importance of kind, loving families is growing, and diverse responses to violence are proliferating. These include public service messages about parenting skills, church-sponsored marital and premarital counseling, peace curricula in the schools, neighborhood watches, and anti-domestic violence initiatives by government and private organizations.

The situation in many areas of the world is not completely analogous to that in the U.S., however. Even though family relationships may be strong, when children grow up experiencing violent attacks on their communities by "the other side," it is difficult for them not to see the attackers as enemies against whom retaliation is not only appropriate but necessary. Constant exposure to violence in early years teaches children that violence is acceptable and effective.

A widespread effort to soften propensities toward aggressive behavior seems impossible to bring about, but failing to do so will only escalate the use of violence as the primary means to an end. Such an effort must involve diverse social entities including families, neighborhoods, schools, communities, governments, religious organizations, and the media if it is to have the necessary global and ongoing effect of decreasing the probability that individuals will develop the thought patterns related to becoming violent.

CONCLUSION

We have addressed several aspects of group violence, viewed it through the lens of terrorism, and formulated three patterns of thinking that contribute to terrorism. One of the most salient conclusions to be drawn from this work is that the difficulty of achieving a peaceful world is enormous, even overwhelming, but the necessity is compelling. Clearly it is idealistic to believe that peaceful means can be substituted for violence everywhere and in every situation. Nevertheless, we believe that individuals and societies must not lose sight of this objective. Ultimately, our best hope may be that each of us keeps as a reference point the desire to see others as human; to learn the many skills involved in maintaining peaceful interactions; to make the effort to achieve our objectives peacefully; to teach peacemaking to our families and others whose lives we touch; and to participate as fully as possible in the development and maintenance of social systems that support humane and compassionate behavior.

REFERENCES

Adams, J. (1986). *The financing of terror: How the groups that are terrorizing the world get the money to do it*. New York: Simon & Schuster.

Atkinson, J. W. (1964). *An introduction to motivation*. Princeton, NJ: C. van Nostrand.

Avrich, P. (1984). *The Haymarket tragedy*. Princeton, NJ: Princeton University Press.

Ballif, B. L. (1977, April). *A multidimensional model of motivation for learning*. Paper presented at the meeting of the American Educational Research Association, New York.

Bandura, A. (1986). *Social foundations of thought and actions: A social cognitive theory*. Englewood Cliffs, NJ: Prentice-Hall.

Bandura, A. (1990). Mechanisms of moral disengagement. In W. Reich (Ed.), *Origins of terrorism: Psychologies, ideologies, theologies, states of mind* (pp. 161-191). Cambridge, UK: Cambridge University Press.

Bassiouni, M. C. (1987). Terrorism, law enforcement, and the mass media: Perspectives, problems, proposals. *Journal of Criminal Enforcement Bulletin, 56,* 14-17.

Begin, M. (1977). *The revolt* (S. Katz, Trans.). Los Angeles: Nash.

Bergen, P. L. (2001a). The bin Laden Trial: What did we learn? *Studies in Conflict and Terrorism, 24,* 429-434.

Bergen, P. L. (2001b). *Holy war, inc.: Inside the secret world of Osama bin Laden*. New York: The Free Press.

Blumenfeld, L. (2002). *Revenge: A story of hope*. New York: Simon & Schuster.

Botsis, J. A., Plutchick, R., Kotler, M., & van Praag, H. M. (1995). Parental loss and family violence as correlates of suicide and violence risk. *Suicide and Life-Threatening Behavior, 25,* 253-260.

Celozzi, M. J., Kazelskis, R., & Gutsch, K. U. (1981). The relationship between viewing televised violence in ice hockey and subsequent levels of personal aggression. *Journal of Sport Behavior, 4,* 157-162.

Centre for National Security Studies (1995). *Recent trends in domestic and international terrorism* [On-line]. Available at: http://www.nsi.org/library/terrorism/tertrend/html

Clayton, C. J., Barlow, S. H., & Ballif-Spanvill, B. (1999). Principles of group violence with a focus on terrorism. In H. V. Hall & L. C. Whitaker (Eds.), *Collective violence: Effective strategies for assessing and interviewing in fatal group and institutional aggression* (pp. 277-311). Boca Raton, FL: CRC Press.

Cooper, H. H. A. (1974). *Evaluating the terrorist threat: Principles and applied risk assessment*. Gaithersburg, MD: International Association of Police Chiefs.

Crenshaw, M. (1981). The causes of terrorism. *Comparative Politics, 13,* 379-399.

Crenshaw, M. (1985). *The strategic development of terrorism*. Paper presented at the annual meeting of the American Political Science Association, New Orleans, LA.

Crenshaw, M. (1990). The logic of terrorism: Terrorist behavior as a product of strategic choice. In W. Reich (Ed.), *Origins of terrorism: Psychologies, ideologies, theologies, states of mind* (pp. 7-24). Cambridge, UK: Cambridge University Press.

Diener, E. (1977). Deindividuation: Causes and consequences. *Social Behavior and Personality, 5,* 143-155.

Diener, E., Dineen, J., Endresen, K., Beaman, A. L., & Fraser, S. C. (1975). Effects of altered responsibility, cognitive set, and modeling on physical aggression and deindividuation. *Journal of Personality and Social Psychology, 31*, 328-337.

Doyle, R. (2001, June). The American terrorist. *Scientific American*, 28.

Fabick, S. D. (in press). Us & them: Reducing the risk of terrorism. In C. E. Stout (Ed.), *The psychology of terrorism: Psychological dimensions to war and peace.* Westport, CT: Praeger Publishers.

Federal Bureau of Investigation (1997). Terrorism: The year in review [On-line]. Available at: http://www.fbi.gov/publish/terror/terrorin.htm

Goodall, J. (1986). *The chimpanzees of Gombe: Patterns of behavior.* Cambridge, MA: Harvard University Press.

Goodall, J., Bandura, A., Bermann, E., Busse, C., Matama, H., Mpongo, E., Pierce, A., & Riss, D. (1979). Inter-community interactions in the chimpanzee population of the Gombe National Park. In D. A. Hamburg & E. R. McCown (Eds.), *The great apes* (pp. 13-53). Menlo Park, CA: Cummings.

Haney, C., Banks, C., & Zimbardo, P. (1973). Interpersonal dynamics in a simulated prison. *International Journal of Criminology and Penology, 1*, 69-97.

Hatfield, E., Cacioppo, J. T., & Rapson, R. L. (1993). Emotional contagion. *Current Directions in Psychological Science, 2*, 96-99.

Heise, D. R., & O'Brien, J. (1993). Emotion expression in groups. In J. M. Haviland & M. Lewis (Eds.), *Handbook of emotions* (pp. 489-497). New York: The Guilford Press.

Heskin, K. (1980). *Northern Ireland: A psychological analysis.* New York: Columbia University Press.

Hoffman, B. (1995). Holy terror: The implications of terrorism motivated by a religious imperative. *Studies in Conflict and Terrorism, 18*, 271-284.

Hoffman, B. (1999). Inside terrorism. New York: Columbia University Press.

Hudson, R. A. (1999). *The sociology and psychology of terrorism: Who becomes a terrorist and why?* Washington, DC: Federal Research Division, Library of Congress.

Janis, I. (1982). *Groupthink: Psychological studies of policy decisions and fiascoes.* (2nd ed.). Boston: Houghton Mifflin.

Keegan, J. (1976). *The face of battle.* Middlesex, UK: Penguin.

Kernberg, O. (1992, February). *The effects of the narcissistic leader on the group.* Paper presented at the American Group Psychotherapy Association Annual Meeting, Atlanta.

Laqueur, W. (1977). *Terrorism.* Boston: Little, Brown.

Lawler, E. J. (1992). Affective attachments to nested groups: A choice process theory. *American Sociological Review, 57*, 327-339.

Levitt, G. M. (1988). Democracies against terror: The western response to state-supported terrorism. *Washington Papers No. 134* (pp. 93-105). New York: Praeger.

Lewis, C. W. (2000). The terror that failed: Public opinion in the aftermath of the bombing in Oklahoma City. *Public Administration Review, 60*, 201-210.

Long, D. E. (1990). *The anatomy of terrorism.* New York: The Free Press.

Manson, J. H., & Wrangham, R. W. (1991). Intergroup aggression in chimpanzees and humans. *Current Anthropology, 32*, 369-390.

Masters, J. C., Felleman, E. S., & Barden, R. C. (1981). Experimental studies of affective states in children. In B. Lahey & A. E. Kazdin (Eds.), *Advances in clinical child psychology* (Vol. 4) (pp. 91-114). New York: Plenum.

McGuire, M. (1973). *To take arms: My year with the IRA Provisionals*. New York: Viking.

Meichenbaum, D., & Gilmore, J. B. (1984). The nature of unconscious processes: A cognitive-behavioral perspective. In K. Bowers & D. Meichenbaum (Eds.), *The unconscious reconsidered* (pp. 273-298). New York: Wiley.

Milgram, S. (1974). *Obedience to authority: An experimental view*. New York: Harper & Row.

Miller, J., Engelberg, S., & Broad, W. (2001). *Germs*. New York: Simon & Schuster.

Monroe, K. R., & Kreidie, L. H. (1997). The perspective of Islamic fundamentalists and the limits of rational choice theory. *Political Psychology, 18*, 19-43.

Morarji, K. (2002, spring). Anti-terrorist legislation: A pretext for attacks on civil liberties around the world. *The Peace Chronicle*, 9-10.

Nishida, T., Hiraiwa-Hasegawa, M., Hasegawa, T., & Takahata, Y. (1985). Group extinction and female transfer in wild chimpanzees in the Mahale National Park, Tanzania. *Zeitschrift fur Tierpsychologie, 67*, 284-301.

Otterbein, K. F. (1970). *The evolution of war*. New Haven: HRAF Press.

Patterson, J. D. (1991). Comment on J. H. Manson & R. W. Wrangham, Intergroup aggression in chimpanzees and humans. *Current Anthropology, 32*, 382.

Pierce, W. L. (1978). *The Turner diaries*. Washington, DC: The National Alliance.

Pomerantz, S. L. (1987). The FBI and terrorism. *FBI Law and Criminology, 72*, 1-51.

Post, J. (1984). Notes on a psychodynamic theory of terrorist behavior. *Terrorism, 7*, 241-256.

Post, J. M. (1990). Terrorist psycho-logic: Terrorist behavior as a product of psychological forces. In W. Reich (Ed.), *Origins of terrorism: Psychologies, ideologies, theologies, states of mind* (pp. 25-40). Cambridge, UK: Cambridge University Press.

Post, J. M., Ruby, K. G., & Shaw, E. D. (2002a). The radical group in context: 1. An integrated framework for the analysis of group risk for terrorism. *Studies in Conflict and Terrorism, 25*, 73-100.

Post, J. M., Ruby, K. G., & Shaw, E. D. (2002b). The radical group in context: 2. Identification of critical elements in the analysis of risk for terrorism by radical group type. *Studies in Conflict and Terrorism, 25*, 101-126.

Prino, C. T., & Peyrot, M. (1994). The effect of child physical abuse and neglect on aggressive, withdrawn, and prosocial behavior. *Child Abuse and Neglect, 18*, 871-884.

Ranstorp, M. (1996). Terrorism in the name of religion. *Journal of International Affairs, 50*, 41-62.

Rasch, W. (1979). Psychological dimensions of political terrorism in the Federal Republic of Germany. *International Journal of Law and Psychiatry, 2*, 79-85.

Reich, W. (1990). Understanding terrorist behavior: The limits and opportunities of psychological inquiry. In W. Reich (Ed.), *Origins of terrorism: Psychologies, ideologies, theologies, states of mind* (pp. 261-279). Cambridge, UK: Cambridge University Press.

Ross, J. I. (1993). Structural causes of oppositional political terrorism: Towards a causal model. *Journal of Peace Research, 30*, 317-329.

Russell, C. A., & Miller, B. H. (1983). Portrait of a terrorist. In L. Freedman & Y. Alexander (Eds.), *Perspectives on terrorism* (pp. 45-60). Wilmington, DE: Scholarly Resources.

Savinkov, B. (1931). *Memoirs of a terrorist* (J. Shaplen, Trans.). New York: A & C Boni.

Scheidlinger, S. (1994). A commentary on adolescent group violence. *Child Psychiatry and Human Development, 25,* 3-11.

Spanish National UNESCO Commission (1986). *Seville Statement on Violence.* Seville, Spain: Author.

Sprinzak, E. (1998). *From theory to practice: Developing early warning indicators for terrorism.* Washington, DC: USIP.

Sternberg, R. J. (2002, August). *A duplex theory of hate and its development and its application to terrorism, massacres, and genocide.* Paper presented at the American Psychological Association conference in Chicago.

Tarvis, C. (1982). *Anger: The misunderstood emotion.* New York: Simon & Schuster.

Tedeschi, J. T., & Felson, R. B. (1994). *Violence, aggression, and coercive actions.* Washington, DC: American Psychological Association.

Terrorism Research Center (1997). *The basics of terrorism* [On-line]. Available at: http://www.terrorism.com/terrorism.bpart1.htm

Title 33, United States Code, Section 2656f(d).

U.S. Department of State (1988). *Patterns of global terrorism.* Washington, DC: U.S. Government Printing Office.

U.S. Department of State (1996). *Patterns of global terrorism.* Washington, DC: U.S. Government Printing Office.

U.S. Department of State (2002). *Patterns of global terrorism.* Washington, DC: U.S. Government Printing Office.

Vogel, W., & Lazare, A. (1990). The unforgivable humiliation: A dilemma in couples' treatment. *Contemporary Family Therapy, 12,* 139-151.

White, R. K. (1968). *Nobody wanted war: Misperception in Vietnam and other wars.* Garden City, NY: Doubleday.

Wilson, E. (1975). *Sociobiology.* Cambridge, MA: Harvard University Press.

Yacef, S. (1962). *Souvenirs de la bataille d'Alger.* Paris: Julliard.

Zawodny, J. K. (1978). Internal organizational problems and the sources of tensions of terrorist movements as catalysts of violence. *Terrorism, 1,* 277-285.

Chemical and Biological Violence: Predictive Patterns in State and Terrorist Behavior

David M. Paltin

SUMMARY. This article describes a rising trend of chemical and biological weapons use among terrorist and rogue state groups. The author notes that, similar to the behavior of the perpetrator and victim in cases of interpersonal violence, predictive patterns begin to emerge when we study the behavior of terrorist groups or rogue leaders accused of using such weaponry. Due to the nature of chemical and biological arms, patterns of behavior occur over months or years prior to actual use. Citing the *Lethal Violence Sequence* as a unit of study, the article observes features of group baseline, pre-conflict, lethal event and recovery behavior that often accompany these attacks. Similar to other acts of genocidal killing, group history with regard to ethnonationalism, mass persecution, and hiding of atrocities become positive predictors of chemical weapons use. *[Article copies available for a fee from The Haworth Document Delivery Service: 1-800-HAWORTH. E-mail address: <docdelivery@haworthpress.com> Website: <http://www.HaworthPress.com> © 2003 by The Haworth Press, Inc. All rights reserved.]*

KEYWORDS. Terrorism, biological weapons, chemical weapons, violence

David M. Paltin, PhD, is affiliated with Orange Psychiatric Associates, Orange, CA.
Address correspondence to: David Paltin, PhD, 173-B North Glassell, Orange, CA 92866.

[Haworth co-indexing entry note]: "Chemical and Biological Violence: Predictive Patterns in State and Terrorist Behavior." Paltin, David M. Co-published simultaneously in *Journal of Threat Assessment* (The Haworth Press, Inc.) Vol. 2, No. 3, 2003, pp. 41-68; and: *Terrorism: Strategies for Intervention* (ed: Harold V. Hall) The Haworth Press, Inc., 2003, pp. 41-68. Single or multiple copies of this article are available for a fee from The Haworth Document Delivery Service [1-800-HAWORTH, 9:00 a.m. - 5:00 p.m. (EST). E-mail address: docdelivery@haworthpress.com].

> *"The mass of war propaganda against the use of gas and other chemicals has caused the average citizen to have an unholy fear of such agents."*
>
> –Maerdian, 1930, p. 692

Following the five deaths resulting from inhalation anthrax and related cutaneous anthrax cases, America has been put on notice regarding our vulnerability to weapons of mass destruction and terrorism. Although multiple Federal agencies have been seriously preparing for a large-scale chemical and biological weapons (CW/BW) attack for the past five to seven years, the September of 2001 incidents helped fill the void of data needed to answer questions about means of delivery and access to biological agents. Some of the predictive hypotheses of Federal law enforcement agencies were confirmed: (1) that characteristics of chemical and biological weapons influence the means of the attack, and (2) that vulnerabilities existing in our basic transportation and communication infrastructures help terrorists overcome the problem of delivery and implementation. The September anthrax incidents resembled the Aum Shinrikyo attacks on these points, providing further base rate data on the salient, predictive factors in a CW/BW incident. Interestingly, the selection of discrete targets and the personal tone conveyed by the accompanying, handwritten notes suggest that the incidents resembled the profile of a revenge poisoning more than its similarity to the profile of a terrorist attack.

This article discusses an alternative prediction scheme to typological profiling in dealing with the imminent threat of CW/BW use among terrorist and rogue state groups. Whereas profiling may be useful in capability analysis and early identification of potential perpetrators (Gorman, 2002; Hudson, 1999), it falls short in predicting the actual sequential development and construction of a CW/BW terrorist event. It is noted that, similar to the behavior of the perpetrator and victim in cases of interpersonal violence, predictive patterns begin to emerge when we study the behavior of terrorist groups or rogue leaders accused of using such weaponry. Due to the nature of chemical and biological arms, patterns of behavior occur over months or years prior to actual use. As discussed later in this article, concurrent behavior patterns involving conventional attacks such as car bombings might affect the evolution of a CW/BW attack.

Citing the *lethal violence sequence* as a unit of study, the author observes features of group baseline, pre-conflict, lethal event and recovery behavior that often accompany these attacks. Similar to other acts of genocidal killing during wartime, group history with regard to religious fundamentalism and ethnic dislocation, indiscriminant target selection, and hiding of evidence become positive predictors of chemical weapons use by terrorists. Victim and contextual contributions are also described for each phase of the lethal violence sequence.

As far back as 1969, the United States Department of Defense and other agencies recognized the vulnerability of U.S. cities to chemical and biological terrorism, and a series of exercises were staged to gather data on the defensive options against a biological weapons attack. Remarkably similar to the Tokyo tragedy, one mock drill involved pumping harmless bacteria into street-level subway vents at various locations in New York City (Simon, 1989). Following the introduction of the material, levels of dispersion, wind carry, and potential death counts were calculated. The results of the study indicated that an actual attack would result in a high casualty rate, and that metropolitan police and military officials were incapable of dealing with these types of weapons. More recently, U. S. government agencies participated in Dark Winter, an exercise in which response capabilities were tested for dealing with three simultaneous smallpox outbreaks ("Combating Terrorism," 2001; The Anser Institute, 2002). The Aum Shinrikyo attacks, strikingly similar to the New York subway experiments, proved that these scenarios were indeed possible to carry out. The disturbing feature of the Tokyo subway incident was not the cult's ability to synthesize a lethal dose of the nerve agent sarin, but rather the fact that Aum had been running a chemical weapons research lab with graduate recruits from the Japanese university system for over five years (The Henry L. Stimson Center, 1996; Kaplan & Marshall, 1996). During this period, cult chemists not only synthesized a variety of agents, but also were able to buy weapons technology in the international marketplace. Unlike other chemical weapons incidents perpetrated by the Bader Meinhoff Gang in Germany and Hezbollah in Israel, Aum had synthesized most of its chemical weapons technology without a state sponsor, proving that any terrorist cell with adequate chemical training can gain access to the most lethal, non-atomic weapons of mass destruction known to humankind.

IMPROVING OUR PREDICTIONS OF CW/BW USE

This article focuses on the prediction of CW/BW use by religious and ethnonationalist terrorist groups and "rogue" nations which are most commonly implicated in CW/BW events (Babievsky, 1997; Douglass, 1995). Examining data from documented lethal incidents, I will use the *lethal violence sequence* as a model for understanding common behavioral patterns that precede and follow these events. I will attempt to develop a predictive analog for group or leader behavior in this area, and to demonstrate its preference over methods of "profiling." For example, if a police or Federal Bureau of Investigation (FBI) unit receives intelligence that an identified group was able to acquire biological materials from the American Type Culture Collection (an embarrassing incident which actually occurred in 1985), how could that agency improve their assessment of the risk of an actual attack? This article describes the central role of: (1) group baseline, (2) concurrent sequences, (3) phase of conflict, and (4) post-event recovery information required for making valid predictions. Finally, solutions and recommendations will be presented that will assist in terrorist intervention and interstate conflict resolution, as well as in future research into lethal violence prevention.

DESCRIPTIVE STATISTICS ON RECENT CHEMICAL AND BIOLOGICAL INCIDENTS

Table 1 presents available data on alleged CW/BW incidents that have occurred from 1978 to the present. As predicted by the lethal violence sequence, the data suggest that some perpetrators of CW incidents were also past offenders. The table also presents the difficulty in gaining accurate casualty data following CW/BW incidents. This difficulty is typically due to regional instability that is the context for many incidents. For example, collection of casualty data on Soviet use of chemicals in Afghanistan was only possible long after the alleged attacks took place due to tribal battles in the area, and casualty data from the Sverdlosk anthrax outbreak was hampered by Soviet information controls (Brookmeyer, Blades, Hugh-Jones, & Henderson, 2001). Terrorists also appear to be underrepresented in the data on successful CW/BW events. This observation does not imply that terrorist groups are less likely candidates to perpetrate an attack. The anthrax incidents of October 2001 notwithstanding, several other "near incidents" have taken place over the past 20 years.

WHO IS MORE LIKELY TO USE CW/BW WEAPONS: EXISTING MODELS FOR PREDICTION

Having the ability to predict which fundamentalist group or rogue leader might use CW/BW technology should be a primary concern of

TABLE 1. Descriptive Statistics on Recent Chemical and Biological Incidents

Incident	Perpetrator Classification	Casualties [A]	Source of Data
1975-80 Vietnamese use of multiple CW agents against Laotian Hmong resistance and Kampuchean army.	Rogue nation w/state sponsors.	Fatalities unknown. Medical reports of 100-300 affected.	Eyewitness and physician report. Medical data.
1979-80 Soviet Union use of unknown CW agents against Afghanistan mujahidin.	Rogue nation.	No accurate data available.	Eyewitness and U.S. State Dept.
1980-1985 Iraqi use of phosgene, mustard and cyanide against Iran.	Rogue nation w/state sponsors.	No accurate data available.	Eyewitness, soil, and medical data.
1985 Rajneesh cult dumping of Salmonella in Oregon reservoir to influence local elections.	Religious group.	50-100 affected.	Forensic and medical data.
1987 Libyan use of unknown CW agents against Chad.	Rogue nation w/state sponsors.	No accurate data available.	U.S. State Dept.
1991 Iraqi use of mustard against town of Nafaj, Iraq.	Rogue nation.	"Most died shortly thereafter," 300-500 affected.	Department of Defense. Eyewitness.
1991 Gulf War troops report suspicion of CW/BW weapons use and exhibit symptoms of Gulf War illnesses.	Rogue Nation. (In wartime context).	49,000-100,000 reporting one or more symptoms. Unconfirmed monitoring report of 4,400 deaths.	Eyewitness. Physical/ biological evidence.
1993 Iraqi dumping CW agents in marshlands, killing Marsh Kurds.	Rogue nation.	Unconfirmed allegations of "hundreds" of fatalities.	Department of Defense.
1993 Bosnian Muslims' use of chlorine gas against Serbian forces.	Ethno-Nationalist group.	No accurate data available. 3 attacks alleged.	United Nations. Eyewitness.
1995 Aum Shinrikyo use of sarin in Japan subways.	Religious cult.	12 fatalities, 5000 affected.	Video data. Eyewitness.
2001 Post mailings containing "weaponized" anthrax spores.	Unknown.	5 fatalities	Forensic and medical data.

[A]Unconfirmed U.S. State Department reports have noted casualty rate of attacks on Kampuchea, Laos and Afghanistan to total 10,000.

national defense and domestic law enforcement agencies. A number of studies have examined individual factors that contribute to an accurate prediction model (Kellen, 1979; McNitt, 1995; Roberts, 1987; Robinson, 1991), although many of these studies were conducted to analyze specific instances of weapons stockpiling by a particular regime or in preparation of an offensive, wartime action. In general, these analyses fall into three basic categories: (1) analyses of characteristics of the weapons themselves and the capability of groups to use them, (2) prediction based on the stages of conflict, and (3) studies of the behavior of "actors" of genocidal violence, including studies of rogue leaders and terrorist groups. Although the first two areas of study will be briefly reviewed, this article suggests that prediction is improved by adding the study of behavioral sequencing to profiling efforts. While profiling is best suited for identification of possible perpetrator groups, behavioral sequence analysis increases our ability to predict readiness and time frames for an impending attack.

Prediction Based on Weapon Characteristics and Capability Analysis

Capability analyses combine scientific data on chemical and biological weapons properties with intelligence about the characteristics, size, and organizational level of potential weapons users. Mengel (1979) pointed out that terrorist attacks involving high-technology weapons require a skilled, team effort. These attacks not only involve implementation of a sophisticated plan, but also acquisition of chemical and weapon delivery materials and storage capability. Rogue states and larger terrorist organizations were believed to be more likely to carry out a large, urban-center attack, whereas smaller groups would be limited in their ability to deliver a large load of chemical or biological material to its target. The anthrax attacks in October of 2001 reduced the relevance of this factor because terrorists do not require sophisticated delivery and production systems when the casualty rate is not the primary goal of the attack. The use of specialized terrorist cells developed to handle chemical or biological weapons might prefer smaller, redundant attacks toward significant, symbolic human targets. The Department of Defense's "Dark Winter" exercise follows this revised opinion ("Combating Terrorism," 2001). Hyman (personal communication, September 22, 1995) astutely pointed out that a determined chemical terrorist can fashion a storage facility out of trash containers in a household bathroom.

Prediction of Events Based on Stages of Conflict

The second area of study in CW/BW violence prediction seeks to reveal the stages or levels of inter-group conflict and aggression. Many violent interstate conflicts or wars follow similar patterns of escalation, from declarations of unfairness and historical claims, to phases of pre-hostility and post-hostility engagement (Brockner & Rubin, 1985; Clarke, 1993; Leng & Singer, 1988). An entirely different set of patterns exists for situations involving terrorists and other anti-government groups who may be less reactive to world opinion. Understanding these commonalities in conflict can help us predict when non-conventional weapons might be employed and, likewise, misjudgments in the stages of conflict can lead to a lack of preparation for a chemical or biological attack. In an interesting review of interstate aggression, Leng (1994) identified the most common types of research study in this field: (1) case studies, (2) "rational choice" and game theory analyses, and (3) quantitative review of event data. Different game rules are present, Leng suggested, at different stages of engagement. For example, in the later stages of conflict a warring state will often choose a riskier offensive option (e.g., non-conventional weapons) if it perceives that it is time to "turn the tide" of battle. Also important in the field of biological and chemical weapons prediction is an understanding of zero-sum thinking: a phenomenon that occurs when a warring entity uses its "final option" in an already lost battle simply to boost the suffering of the opponent. The U.S. decision to increase its use of Napalm and other chemical desiccants in North Vietnam during the final weeks of war might be considered an example of zero-sum thinking, as were Hitler's orders to send troops into the streets of Berlin when it was clear that defeat was at hand.

Clarke's (1993) "rational" model of conflict prediction and termination offers a thorough description of different stages of conflict, as well as dynamic mechanisms that trigger changes from one level of conflict to another. The decision of one side to change the level of hostilities often occurs when that side changes its initial objectives. For example, during the pre-hostility phase of the Gulf War, Saddam Hussein decided to place a group of British citizens under what he euphemistically termed "protective custody" which served to increase the probability of hostile conflict with the United States. Hussein thus changed his initial objective of holding Kuwait to include the collection of human "bargaining chips" that might help prevent active bombing of military targets. Clarke suggested that the correct strategy in dealing with changes in phases of hostility is to change the objectives of one's opponent and to reduce an opponent's "will to resist." In dealing with a chemical or biological threat, this means either increasing the negative consequences a group might suffer for using such weapons or by distracting an opponent with another objective. When U.S. intelligence officials correctly predicted a phase transition as Hussein moved chemical and biological munitions to the lines of battle, a message was sent to Baghdad indicating that the U.S. would turn the sands of Iraq into "a glass parking lot" with tactical nuclear weapons if chemicals or biologicals were used. Defense officials later claimed that this threat effectively reduced the desirability of the Iraqi regime to utilize their chemical weapons (Department of Defense, 1990b).

Predicting the Behavior of the Actor

Whereas capability analyses and technical reviews stand as the "case studies" of chemical and biological violence, analyzing the actor or perpetrator of lethal CW/BW incidents follows the trend toward increased use of profiling in violence prediction and prevention. The popularity of profiling is likely due more to the development of computer database systems such as the Interstate Identification Index (I.I.I.) than on actual rates of success in profiling cases (Department of Justice, 2001). The rationale for profiling is that "most terrorists have common characteristics that can be determined through psychometric analysis of large quantities of biographical data on terrorists" (Hudson, 1999, p. 11). The following qualities and identifying characteristics of groups may be suggestive of a greater likelihood of CW/BW violence:

Group solidarity. Generally, terrorist groups with strong solidarity are more likely to engage in violent behavior than less cohesive groups. As Post (1990) suggested, cohesive groups can adeptly magnify the emotional cues underlying their members' behavior, quickly becoming a "psychologically unstable group that functions as an emotional hothouse" (p. 67). Research has not yet specified whether solidarity offers a direct link to non-conventional violence, whether it acts indirectly by discouraging dissenting communication, or through some combination of these factors.

Group sponsorship by another CW/BW nation. Alexander (1994) and Spiers (1994) indicated that sponsorship by other countries increases the potential threat of terrorist and rogue groups. Covert transfers of chemical and biological precursors and intelligence through military advisors boost the technological capability of groups, while increasing their confidence by the support of a larger state entity. Often, these transfers appear as sales of "agricultural supplies" or "medical products" between legitimate businesses and foreign states which allow sponsor nations to deny their participation if questioned by the world body. In 1989, the CIA described to Congress a series of transactions that had taken place between German manufacturers and Libyan buyers during construction of the Rabta Chemical Plant. Though state complicity was denied, it was suggested that Bundestag officers might have looked aside to avoid calling attention to the transactions. Similar accusations were made against the U.S. Department of Commerce after the end of the Gulf War when it was revealed that Iraq received nearly 10 to 20 shipments of biological "dual use" materials originating from the American Type Culture Collection under the guise of agricultural development (Arming Iraq, 1994).

The dangerous leader. Although often misused as political propaganda, the identification of the dangerous leader may be useful in differentiating chemically armed-and-willing rogue states from their benign counterparts (Aragno, 1991). Mayer (1993) defined the dangerous leader as having "a low level of connection to other people and high proneness to violence. Other traits are an intolerance of criticism and a grandiose sense of national entitlement. Dangerous leaders murder advisors and citizens, condone torture, are intolerant of the press, feel superior, increase their militaries, and use secret police actions" (p. 331).

"Lone wolf" perpetrators. Culminating with suspicions that the October, 2001 anthrax incidents were perpetrated by a domestic terrorist or American citizen (Berlau, 2002; MacKenzie, 2002), the FBI developed a profile of a domestic bioterror perpetrator that included characteristics such as: male, Caucasian, possessing technical or biochemical training and experience, with previous government or military work experience. This profile appeared to be based on generalizations from domestic radicals using conventional weaponry, as well as experiences with individuals who have threatened to use biological weapons. As with other profiles extrapolated from the assumed motivation of the perpetrator, sparse base rate data limits the predictive strength of the "lone wolf" profile. Although a disgruntled individual might design and unleash a biological or chemical weapons attack, history and capability analysis suggests that a poisoning event would be more likely than a wide-scale, airborne event with mass casualties.

Religiously inspired and fundamentalist religious groups. Religious identification offers a complex scheme of motivations and justifications that can be played out in the midst of national or civil conflict.

State-sponsored religious beliefs can serve to relieve participants of guilt and victim empathy. End-world thinking and promises of post-suicide utopia reduce the inhibitory factors that limit the behavior of other types of perpetrators. In a study of 60 communal genocides that occurred around the world since 1945, Harff and Gurr (1989) found that groups at highest risk for genocide are most heavily concentrated in the Middle East region where there has been an upsurge in both religious fundamentalist acceptance and chemical and biological weapons proliferation (Alexander, 1994; Shultz & Schmauder, 1994). Although radical Islamic groups accounted for a small percentage of terrorist attacks as of 2001, they were responsible for a disproportionate number of effective, high-casualty attacks (Johnson, 2001).

Ethnonationalist groups and regimes. A number of authors have described the link between mass killing and ethnic-based nationalist movements (Hagopian, 1978; Horowitz, 1985; Kellen, 1979). Ethnonationalism combines ethnic identification with themes of historical dislocation and persecution (Lifton, 1976, 1982; Lifton & Falk, 1982; Lifton & Markusen, 1990). Shultz and Schmauder (1994) noted that in ethnonationalist conflict "atrocities are frequent," and that "usual conventions of war are ignored" (p. 5). Lifton suggested that a *totalistic ideological response* guides actors in ethnonationalist regimes, in which individuals or group cells within a society try to develop new "meaning structures" that will ease their sense of historical dislocation. Often, this response carries with it the theme of finding a "cure" which will purge society of its "illness." The regime identifies certain individuals, organizations, or peoples as the "disease" which caused the group illness. The cure for the disease becomes the genocidal elimination of large groups of people.

Using Behavioral Analysis to Develop a CW/BW Lethal Violence Sequence

Margolin (1977) recommended leaving behind the contradictory psychological and motivational theories that have dominated the field of terrorist studies to understand the use of CW/BW. Behavioral analysis offers an alternative to motivational or demographic profiling for the purposes of actually predicting a CW/BW or terrorist event (Wilson, 2000). Whereas profiling may be a helpful method for accumulating a list of "usual suspects," systems of behavioral analysis take the next step to identify patterns of behavior that might signal an impending CW/BW attack. The *lethal violence sequence* detailed in this article provides the theoretical groundwork for this approach. The method is analogous to the "police blotter" type of criminal detection in which law enforcement agents would look for suspicious patterns of events or behavior in a geographic area or among individuals with criminal histories. The FBI's intention to canvas American flight schools emphasized this type of analytical method, as well as monitoring financial behavior of known terrorist groups.

In the behavioral perspective, patterns of group behavior, behavioral histories, and other observant data take precedence over group motivational states and group and leader psychology. The emphasis remains focused on details of the actor's past and present activity—Have past target selections been random or specific? Is the group currently engaged in a practicing phase against a selected target? Have there been attempts to cover up evidence of biological or chemical research? In other cases, the approach may be used to study a set of data not yet linked to a potential perpetrator, for example, by analyzing patterns and types of inquiries received by university biology departments about pathogens. Finally, as pointed out by Hall (1996), a clear understanding of lethal violence, whether genocidal or interpersonal, requires attention to the contributions of the victim and context in the scheme of the event. It is not enough to know only the perpetrator's motivations and behavior. For this reason, sections on context and victim behavior are also included in this review.

As illustrated in the following description of the CW/BW lethal violence sequence, common behavioral patterns emerge when we examine not only the violent event, but also early and late stages of enactment. Readers will note similarities in the sequence of internal/emotional and behavioral events that take place in a chemical weapons incident compared to behaviors we might observe with other violent perpetrators such as participants in genocides and paramilitary operations.

The Lethal Violence Sequence for CW/BW Weapons Use

Measuring the group baseline. The group baseline provides the starting point for understanding the progression to later stages of the lethal violence sequence. The baseline, more commonly associated with single-subject or single-behavior research, is a frequency measurement of identified behavioral targets (Bootzin, Acocella, & Alloy, 1993). Although it may be helpful to have access to a complete behavioral dossier of a terrorist cell or rogue state leader's past use of violence, only particular aspects of prior behavior are relevant to our purpose of identifying the preliminary stages of CW/BW use. Based on the author's review of actual CW/BW incidents and relevant literature, the following types of behavioral data provide information related to later CW/BW behaviors:

1. Prior acts of violence that have been directed toward random (i.e., general population) rather than discriminating targets.
2. Prior attacks that have included detailed planning and rehearsal.
3. Group or rogue state has previously used "sophisticated" weaponry or any type of weapon of mass destruction, or, group has had involvement in food or water poisonings.
4. Group or state has been accused of actively seeking to purchase CW/BW materials.
5. Prior attacks that have resulted in mass casualties.
6. Prior attacks that did not include "red letter" warnings (i.e., attacks not preceded by anonymous notes or telephone warnings).
7. Group or rogue state has engaged in "ethnic purges" or genocidal programs sanctioned by governing body.
8. Past genocidal killings were followed by official denials or hiding of evidence.

Cell division, the assignment of "specialist" research or attack cells within a perpetrator group by the group hierarchy, may also be a feature of terrorist or rogue state development that predates later stages of CW/BW lethal violence. Cells are developed based on a number of factors including a need to maintain secrecy about a CW/BW program from other members of the group, the need to increase research and specialized knowledge, and the need to focus certain "hardcore" individuals in research or attack preparation. Like any organization trying to implement a plan, cell division is a utilitarian decision. With the Rajneesh poisonings (see Table 1), for example, cell division involved a small subgroup that included an executive ruling member of the cult and another individual who could contribute expertise in biology and had access to pathogens.

Victim contributions. Chemical and biological terrorism within American borders had occurred prior to the October, 2001 anthrax mailings and this form of terrorism is likely to remain a part of our future. For example, Bowman (1994, p. 142) cited the 1984 case against a White supremacist group which was planning to dump 200 gallons of cyanide into main reservoirs of Chicago, New York, or Washington, DC. Why does the public distance itself from the recognition of living within a chemically and biologically vulnerable environment? Why do we err in our risk analysis of an impending attack when in retrospect the data seem to have cried out for attention? Paltin (1990) completed a study of public reaction to the threat of nuclear holocaust, including psychological influences that insulate people who are living under such a threat. One significant finding emerged from this study: people often experience a sense of narcissistic invulnerability, what we might term "selfism," as a common reaction to thinking about and imagining a nuclear event. In other words, participants in the study exhibited a counter-phobic psychological defense of self-preservation, an experience of being invincible to annihilation from this type of mass destruction. It is possible that, as potential victims, the public and law-enforcement agencies alike maintain this defense in reaction to the threat of chemical and biological attack. During the baseline phase, we might describe the victim's contribution to the approaching event as one of direct or indirect choice-making regarding chemical and biological security. It is interesting to compare American apathy on the topic with the response of citizens of Israel, where prevention and monitoring of terrorism are an active part of civic responsibility for each citizen.

Contextual features. In the case of both terrorist and rogue state violence, context contributes to the situation in our failure to recognize and act upon cues or patterns of violent or threatening behavior. We do not confront what we see. Although the State Department, in cooperation with the Department of Defense, the CIA, and the FBI, maintains current reports on potential "hot spots" across the nation and around the globe, taking preventative action against a rogue state based on baseline data alone does not often occur. Concerns about political and diplomatic pressure act as inhibitors to taking a proactive stand against countries that have a history of genocidal violence or are known to be developing chemical and biological weapons programs. Political history, beginning with the Geneva treaty of 1925 and up to a more recent CW/BW anti-proliferation agreement finally ratified by the U.S. Congress in 1997, shows us that despite the seeming rationality of a program to prohibit and eliminate stockpiling of chemical and biological weapons, debate about the usefulness and need for such weapons continues.

The Pre-Conflict Phase

Weapons research and acquisition. The first stage of the pre-conflict phase involves the acquisition of chemical and biological weapons technology and materials. This stage may occur months or years before the group decides to actually use the weapons in an attack, or before a target is selected. As noted earlier in this article, germ spores such as anthrax, or chemical elements such as fertilizers or vesicants are easily obtained from a variety of underground and "legitimate" sources. During this phase, a group will often aggressively seek an assortment of materials rather than focusing their efforts on a single substance (Timmerman, 1991). Acquisition is also followed by the installation of a "research program," through which the group members increase their familiarity with different areas of weapons use. The goal of the group members in this stage is to increase their capability to utilize what they have acquired, and to maintain secrecy about their operations. Schools for training and research for military personnel are established at this stage; for example, larger schools include Russia's "Red Banner Academy of Chemical Defense," or the United States' "Army Chemical School."

Bargaining for demands. Near-entry into the lethal violence phase of the sequence is often characterized by a group's attempts to engage a potential target or government in bargaining for certain political demands or favors. As noted by Mengel (1979, p. 208), vague, universalistic demands such as "overthrow of the oppressors," "peace through anarchy," and "restoration of God's will" are more commonly associated with mass violence rather than specific demands such as "restoration of national elections," "releasing political prisoners," and "exposing presidential corruption." Demands may carry the nuance of a justification for mass violence, as we witness the "internal, psychological motivation" for the attack beginning to drive the group's activities. In rare instances where bargaining has been successful, the group will either return to the pre-conflict phase or will submit additional demands.

Selecting the target. Following the rational objective model of terroristic and rogue state behavior, targets for chemical weapons attacks are often selected based on the goals of the group. For a terrorist organization, induction of mass fear in a population might be the desired goal (Simon, 1989), whereas a rogue state leader might be interested in genocidal elimination of dissenting ethnic or regional groups (Stohl, 1984). Target selection also appears to correspond with baseline data on previous acts of violence. An ethnonationalist group that has a history of conflict with a particular ethnic group might be expected to choose that group as a target for chemical attack.

Victim contributions. Unfortunately, victims of chemical and biological violence, whether by terrorist or interstate attack, receive little information during the pre-conflict phase that would allow them to maintain some measure of personal protection and defense. Public notification of an impending bomb threat may take place, but suggestions that chemical or biological weapons might be involved are likely to be kept secret, either to control panic or to maintain public trust. Even soldiers entering a known chemical operations theater are often given disinformation about the threats involved or effectiveness of preventive medications ("Is military research," 1994). Yet information and defensive equipment are both available and could increase the survivability of a chemical or biological incident if used properly. Again, Israel provides an example of a government engaging its citizens in personal prevention efforts during an active CW/BW threat. During the Persian Gulf War, Israel negotiated with the U.S. State Department not to participate actively in the offensive against Iraq as long as the U.S. provided adequate defenses against Iraq's chemical and missile operations (Watson, George, Tsouras, & Cyr, 1993). As a result, Israeli citizens were given masks and protective materials, as well as specific and detailed instructions on the use of gas masks and building protective shelters (Wolfe, personal communication, March 6, 1991). Had a CW-bearing scud attack on Tel Aviv or Haifa occurred, no doubt such preparations would have decreased the resulting rate of casualty.

Contextual features. As Leng (1994) noted, the approach toward the active use of force often increases the resolve of the players involved and promotes risk-taking. Not coincidentally, the accompanying stress of conflict increases misperceptions of threat on both sides, reduces accurate decision-making, and increases cognitive rigidity (Holsti, 1989). As a result, the context of pre-conflict tension may increase the risk of an organization or country deciding to deploy or ready its available CW/BW arms. This state of posturing and miscommunication also prevents active negotiation that might serve to reduce the risk of CW/BW use during interstate conflict. The situation is magnified when dealing with terrorist or cult group threats, where negotiation is discouraged to avoid "legitimizing" the cause of the group. Both the United States and Israel maintain a "no negotiation" policy with regard to terrorists. As a result, the only remaining strategy for discouraging CW/BW use in this phase is to promote the perception that the use of chemical or biological weapons would result in severe retaliation, and would end in the death or life imprisonment of all terrorist or cult members (e.g., a variation of MacNamara's Mutually Assured Destruction policy of the 1960s nuclear era).

Rehearsing the attack. After a decision to perpetrate violence has been made, the lethal violence phase of a CW/BW attack is preceded by a period of active rehearsal and handling of chemical and biological arms. Practice is necessary due to the complexity of the weaponry. With rogue states, rehearsal may consist of chemical drills and exercises designed to familiarize personnel with weapons use, protective gear, and potential dangers. Individual perpetrators will build and test a mock delivery system or walk through a planned dispersion route. Care in use of chemical and biological materials is often a key focus in training and practice, as mishandling of these materials is quickly fatal to participants. During the Gulf War, Saddam Hussein designated "chemical awareness weeks," in which soldiers received additional practice in working with gas masks, hazardous canisters, and other materials. Identifying rehearsal and drill programs can provide valuable information regarding a group's CW/BW capability.

The Lethal Violence Phase

The triggering stimulus. In contrast to the cues that incite violent crime, the identification of a triggering stimulus for a CW/BW event is often quite elusive. However, it is sometimes possible to identify a series of events that contributed to the timing of an attack, for example, following the failure of bargaining rounds, the anniversary of a prior atrocity, or the death of a political prisoner. Familiarity with a group's historical and target identifications may be informative. The important factor is what the group or individual views as a symbolic representation of the target, not our own symbols of identification (for example, Independence Day for the United States). Triggering stimuli include past events which are used by the group as a rationale for their existence or which serve to increase the emotional intensity of the group (Crenshaw, 1992).

In many cases, violent collective entities do not need triggers to aggress as the decision to perpetrate violence may be part of a long-range strategy (Hall, 1996). In these instances, the availability of victims and targets sets the violence into motion, not triggering stimuli.

The actual CW/BW event. Unlike conventional weapons attacks which have the potential to satisfy a terrorist group's hunger with a visual record of an incident in the rubble of a building or an overturned bus, chemical and biological attacks are only successful if they result in human casualty. Mass death, or engaging the opponent's fear of inescapable, noxious death, is the sole emotional payoff of choosing such a complex, hard-to-manage weapon. Due to this fact, potential targets of a chemical or biological weapon are rarely given a warning call or "red letter" prior to the attack in order to prevent human casualty. Once the CW/BW event is underway, it can be assumed that the group has found a sufficient, internal justification for the high lethality of the attack and does not feel obligated to warn potential victims.

The CW/BW event phase can be either a discrete, single event or a series of attacks over the active course of an interstate conflict. However, due to the amount of money, time, and preparation involved in the use of these weapons, single event use appears to be the exception rather than the rule. With regard to prediction, acknowledging that an initial attack may likely be followed with subsequent incidents should allow for increased preparation of potential victims and organization by civil defense or government agencies. We might also expect that a "clustered" attack of simultaneous lethal events would be favored by a terrorist cell with a limited attack time frame, whereas intrastate and wartime use of CW/BW weapons could be extended over months or years, as was the case in the Iran-Iraq war.

Manipulation of the scene following the attack. The end of the lethal violence phase is often signaled by an attempt to reduce the evidence of CW/BW use by its perpetrator. Dismantling and hiding chemical shells, changing locations of research facilities, and mass burials of corpses by military personnel in chemical protective gear, have been reported following past CW/BW incidents. Corresponding to the field of research in genocidal killing, CW/BW perpetrators may engage in this behavior due to fears of violent retribution (Stewart & Zimmerman, 1989), or to avoid angering a state sponsor (Simon, 1989). Due to the brief half-life of compounds such as VX, Soman, and biologicals such as anthrax, and to delays between the reported date of attack and the arrival of an inspection team, hiding physical evidence of an attack is quite feasible even when inspection involves careful soil and air analysis. This situation may lead to confusion between the compelling, multiple eyewitness reports of attacks and the findings of search teams or observers. Without clear physical markers, the finding "unconfirmed" is often the outcome of post-event site inspections.

Victim reaction to the event. The survivors of toxic chemical or biological exposure face the remainder of their lives with a host of debilitating physiological and psychological effects. The physiological damage that occurs from exposure to neurotoxins or biological organisms was described earlier in this article, and can include neurological impairment, dermatological complications, major organ involvement, immunological impairment, and neuromuscular impairment. Less known are the psychological effects of survival, the manifestations of acute stress disorder, post-traumatic stress symptoms, and accompanying depression. One Persian Gulf veteran who manifested symptoms of fibromyalgia, asthma, seizures, and chronic pain following his return described his feelings as follows: "I was healthy before the war. Now I'm 33 years old but I feel like I'm 80 years old inside" (B. Jones, Personal communication, September 9, 1995). The psychological effects of a successful chemical or biological attack extend outward into the community or population whose members were its target, and then expand to the entire human community. Although acts of terrorism, whether chemical or conventional, leave a lasting impression of vulnerability and insecurity in society, the author believes that CW/BW terrorism and genocide are particularly hurtful (DiGiovanni, 1999). For example, there are an abundance of popular hero images that engage our feelings of symbolic immortality. The popular media offers characters to us who can survive explosions, automatic weapons fire, and even alien invasion. The author has encountered no parallel psychohistorical images associated with chemical or biological weapons.

Contextual features which influence the event. The contributions of context during the lethal violence phase are often difficult to discern. Triggering or inhibiting contextual stimuli vary with the type of CW/BW scenario. In terrorist situations, interstate relations between a terrorist surrogate country and a target nation can influence the outcome of a potential lethal event. As Simon (1989) suggested, terrorist groups may be unwilling to go against counter commands of a sponsoring state if the groups wish to maintain the state's sponsorship. Rogue state use of chemical weapons in ethnic genocide or political cleansing might be vulnerable to threats of embargo outside of military intervention, though this level of involvement by outside nations is rare.

Context can also influence the sequence of lethal violence by providing reinforcement for terrorist or rogue leader behavior. For example, if the objective of a terrorist group is to reveal the weakness or vulnerability of a government in protecting its citizens, a successful CW/BW attack becomes the reinforcer for continuation of the lethal violence sequence. If political revenge or economic disruption is the goal, then the threat of mass poisoning can generate the desired result. This was the case with the 1978 Palestinian threat to inject exported Israeli oranges with mercury, as well as the more recent case of poisoning candy from the Morinaga Candy Factory in Japan. In summary, a successful terrorist event is a self-reinforcing activity.

The Recovery Phase

Denial of the incident and expunging of records. The transition to the recovery phase is often marked by increasing statements of denial of participation in the incident, or denials that the incident actually took place. Denials may continue even when evidence to the contrary is readily available. A review of historical CW/BW incidents suggests that this behavior is particularly characteristic of state perpetrators attempting to hide within-state urbanocides on dissenting ethnic groups or political foes. Unlike psychological denial, the motivation attributed to terrorists' denial is to avoid condemnation or retaliation following the incident. However, from a psychosociological perspective, the manipulation and expunging of acts of violence from the historical record might be considered a form of psychic numbing, or as a final stage of "cleansing" and purification as described by Lifton and Falk (1982).

The return to acquisition phase or pre-conflict bargaining. In the final stage of recovery, the terrorist group or state attempts to re-engage in political dialogue and bargaining to continue its normal political process. If sanctions have been imposed by a regional or world council, reducing or eliminating those sanctions becomes the focus of activity. If concern over CW/BW capability remains intense, bargaining over the scope and protocol of external investigations by the World Health Organization or United Nations investigating teams may be included in post-event bargaining (Federation of American Scientists, 1996). A state or terrorist cell may also renew its process of acquisition of CW/BW technology and arms after external attention toward its behavior has died down.

The Important Role of Concurrent Sequences

Large terrorist groups can be expected to have more than one lethal violence sequence according to the type of weapon or attack being utilized. For example, a sophisticated group such as Al-Qaeda had several attack programs being planned at any point in time. Recognizing concurrent sequences offers predictive power in that it suggests that a group may have progressed in different stages among separate lethal violence curves involving conventional or non-conventional weapons. There may be a "staggered" effect in which a group is in the lethal violence or recovery phases of a conventional bomb attack, but has not yet progressed from the pre-conflict, weapons acquisition phase of their CW/BW sequence. As with Al-Qaeda, the implementation of a conventional weapons attack (i.e., using incendiary means to attack a building) on September 11th led to military intervention that interrupted or delayed Al-Qaeda's CW/BW lethal violence sequence. In this manner, the conventional weapons attack led to the "inhibitory variable" of American military intervention. In other less fortunate cases, the implementation of a conventional weapons attack might serve as a trigger to move a group along the lethal violence sequence for bioweapons from a pre-conflict to a lethal violence phase.

CASE VIGNETTE ILLUSTRATING THE CW/BW LETHAL VIOLENCE SEQUENCE

During the violent political rise of Saddam Hussein and the Ba'ath (Renaissance) party in Iraq, a tradition of ethnic violence continued, as Kurdish peoples to the north and independent Shi'ites to the south became the target of acts of government terrorism. During his first years in power, Hussein recognized the strategic power of acquiring chemical and biological weapons technology. He began acquiring CW/BW technology and chemical precursors from a number of private firms located mostly in West Germany, Holland and Italy. Military advisors were also engaged to assist Iraq in its development of chemical technology, opening the Samarra plant in the mid-1980s and other plants at other locations. Iraqi chemical weapons officers were well-schooled in their craft, many having received advanced degrees at training institutes in the Soviet Union (Department of Defense, 1991b). The ease by which Iraq successfully courted a complete CW/BW development campaign from nations who had committed to chemical arms control is chilling, and marked the beginning of a lethal violence sequence that continued for nearly two decades.

Iraq transitioned from its baseline and pre-conflict phases and entered its first active lethal violence phase during the middle years of the Iran-Iraq war. In the early months of the conflict, Iraq suffered massive casualties at the hands of the new messianic Shi'ite state. The Iranians were surprisingly effective in their offenses, and were able to secure territory south of Baghdad. The situation changed drastically in 1984, when Iraq began its chemical offensive against its enemy. Aircraft loaded with sarin and tabun and mortar rounds of mustard and cyanide were used against strategic Iranian facilities and troops ("U.N. Says Iraq," 1988). Wisely predicting that Western nations would maintain political silence during Iraqi chemical offenses and be hypocritical of their prior commitments to chemical treaties, Iran brought its chemical weapons victims to hospitals in New York and Western Europe where the news media would have a firsthand account of the situation (Hughes, 1988). Iraqi chemical weapons attacks against the Iranians either decreased or ended in 1987, already having doubled the casualty rate endured during the war.

In 1988, Iraq entered a pre-conflict phase of its second lethal violence sequence when it renewed its chemical and germ warfare acquisition efforts. Reports of cyanide shipments and development of a germ warfare plant filtered through to the world media. Later in 1988, Hussein held a conference in which he invited Iraqi-born physicists and chemists to return from their studies abroad to work on domestic military projects (Department of Defense, 1990a). Despite these indications of a renewal of Iraq's CW/BW capability, the United States government maintained official silence on the issue, as the press speculated that Washington wished to avoid embarrassment of the Iraqi government ("Iraq said to be," 1989). Later investigation by Congress revealed that the United States had also been exporting shipments of raw chemical and biological materials to Iraq as medical and agricultural development projects ("Arming Iraq," 1994b). These contextual events preceded a new lethal violence phase which Iraq entered in 1990, during the months preceding the Gulf War.

The victims we will identify in this vignette are the Kurdish tribes of the Iraqi Northern border. Indications during the Gulf War that Iraq had entered the lethal violence phase included active rehearsal and practice of CW/BW operations, and public declarations and threats of chemical capability such as, "He who threatens us with an atomic bomb will be annihilated by binary chemicals" ("Iraq Warns," 1990, p. A1).

At the end of the war, Iraqi officials met with its U.S. counterparts under a large canopy set up near Safwan in southern Iraq to discuss the terms of surrender. The United States was adamant about keeping Iraqi fixed-wing aircraft grounded. The U.S. believed it had Iraqi aggression fully contained. The Iraqis asked for permission to fly non-fixed-wing aircraft (helicopters) over outlying Iraqi towns in order to drop medical and food supplies to its citizens. This was an odd request, as it was common knowledge that citizens in these areas had been inciting rebellion against Hussein's regime following the war, and were considered a threat by Baghdad. General Norman Schwartzkopf and the other Americans at the table unwisely agreed, not recognizing that Hussein was, in effect, requesting permission to fly genocidal missions over Kurdish towns in order to secure his territory ("Interview with Rick Atkinson," 1996).

While developing his autocratic regime, Hussein was never able to gain the allegiance of the Kurdish minority who lived primarily outside of Baghdad. The Kurds represented a political and personal, but hardly a military, challenge to Hussein. The American agreement provided the contextual trigger that initiated the following chemical lethal violence event. In the proceeding weeks, reports filtered back from the borders that Iraq had launched a number of helicopter-based chemical weapons attacks against the Kurds. In the town of Nafaj, citizens were herded into vacant lots and told to wait for further instructions. Minutes later, helicopters loaded with sprayers showered the crowd with nitric acid, killing hundreds of men, women, and children (Department of Defense, 1991a). Iraq's well-publicized effort to foil the efforts of the U.N. inspection team identifies the "manipulation of scene" that commonly follows such incidents. Following two cycles of the lethal violence sequence, Iraq reentered a recovery phase in which it has steadfastly denied that it ever used chemical weapons. Unconfirmed reports suggested that Iraq was again searching for CW/BW materials as early as 1992.

RECOMMENDATIONS FOR INTERVENTION IN THE CW/BW LETHAL VIOLENCE SEQUENCE

Although recent efforts to eliminate stockpiling and proliferation are commendable, singular efforts to reverse the growing threat of chemical and biological weapons use will never be effective without the multidimensional participation of individual citizens, national leaders, multinational corporations, and world councils. Solutions must address issues of psychological numbing and ethnonationalist dislocation, as suggested in Lifton's work, and not focus solely on bans and export controls of chemical and biological materials. Prediction efforts by law enforcement and policing agencies must include an understanding of group and leader behavior and, in particular, the characteristics of the CW/BW lethal violence sequence. Utilizing these strategies will increase our ability to practice what Hopple (1993) might term policy with intelligence, using baseline knowledge to guide our decision-making.

Solutions for Individuals Concerned About the Threat of CW/BW Use

Involvement with the activities of groups of professionals that work toward solutions in the CW/BW arena may reduce feelings of vulnerability and helplessness. Inquire about membership in groups that represent rational views on chemical and biological arms. For example, the Federation of American Scientists and Stockholm International Peace Research Initiative (SIPRI) actively research and participate in these issues.

Solutions for Law Enforcement Officials and Federal Antiterrorist Agencies

Law enforcement should learn to identify preparation and baseline phases of a CW/BW lethal violence sequence and their associated behaviors. A file of case examples based on potential scenarios, with suggested interventions that might occur at different phases of the sequence, would assist in training efforts. Law enforcement and field officers should be encouraged to adopt systems of "pattern analysis" and to avoid unhelpful profiling.

The database intelligence approach to terrorist monitoring creates problems in: (1) decentralizing important information, and (2) causing errors in categorizing intelligence items. Existing databases such as the I.I.I. are helpful in monitoring conventional, but not terrorist criminal activity. As law enforcement agencies expand their role to include terrorism prevention, database collections should be reexamined to provide data more relevant to the task at hand.

Manufacturer and Industry Solutions

Industries must monitor large export sales of heavy equipment, aerosol generators, refrigeration systems, and dual-use chemicals and vaccines to countries suspected of having chemical or biological weapons programs. In particular, consider additional consultation with the Department of Commerce for large exports to Ethiopia, Egypt, Israel, South Korea, China, India, Myanmar, Syria, and Pakistan. Industry executives may be mindful of the lessons learned by companies who were involved in sales with the Iraqi government during the 1980s, and who are now facing civil litigation in Texas.

Industry leaders might stimulate new approaches to current issues in global CW/BW proliferation, waste management of chemical stockpiles, and other areas of concern. Encourage original thinking and research in these areas. For example, a large chemical or biomedical research firm might sponsor a conference with a combined faculty drawn from industry researchers and proliferation monitoring groups such as the Federation of American Scientists.

As Kellman (2002) wisely noted, private companies involved in pharmaceutical and agricultural research and manufacturing may fall prey to inefficient federal regulation or oversight of their facilities. Kellman suggested an alternative approach in which biological and pharmaceutical manufacturers partner in monitoring and investigative efforts. Industry leaders could also assist by developing lab control protocols, security systems and standards designed to eliminate "after hours" use of equipment and materials. Efforts should extend to university and college facilities that also maintain the capacity to ferment and weaponize chemical and biological materials.

Government and International Solutions

In determining the CW/BW intentions or capability of a terrorist group or rogue state, increase efforts to collect baseline and group behavioral data that will assist in locating that group within its lethal violence sequence. Do not overvalue deployment and logistical intelligence at the expense of information on patterns of past and recent use of chemical or biological arms, rehearsal and training, or information on a country's history of mass killings or other predictors of CW/BW use.

Ease confidentiality restrictions on export data maintained by the Bureau of Export Administration of the Department of Commerce. Allow and encourage independent, external monitoring of Department of Commerce decisions. Encourage other governments to develop similar policies for export security. Note the example of the successful interdiction of Bull's "supergun" exports from Great Britain to Iraq, which was due to cooperative efforts of both private-sector and government agencies.

Government and agency leaders should recall that most historical, non-combat CW/BW events have involved poisonings rather than airborne delivery of materials. Over-planning for an airborne attack is inconsistent with base rate information on past events. Water and food supply systems represent much more feasible targets than large groups of individuals in an enclosed environment or within a disease epidemic zone.

Psychohistorical dislocation occurs when a community or people undergoes rapid change and social upheaval due to civil war, urban migration and government persecution. Aid programs developed by the Armed Services and State Department should remain micro-sized, stress values of community pride and mutual assistance, and should avoid larger national needs such as highway or power plant rebuilding.

REFERENCES

Alexander, Y. (1994). *Middle East terrorism: Current threats and future prospects.* Hong Kong: Dartmouth.

Aragno, A. (1991). Master of his universe. *Journal of Psychohistory, 19,* 97-108.

Arming Iraq: The export of biological materials and the health of our Gulf War veterans, 103rd Cong., 1st Session (February 9, 1994a).

Arming Iraq: The export of biological materials and the health of our Gulf War veterans, 103rd Cong, 1st Session (February 9, 1994b) (Testimony of R. Riegle).

Babievsky, K. K. (1997). Chemical and biological terrorism. *Low Intensity Conflict and Law Enforcement, 6,* 163-168.

Berlau, J. (2002). Is the FBI following the wrong trail? *Insight on the News, 18,* 16.

Bootzin, R. R., Acocella, J. R., & Alloy, L. B. (1993). *Abnormal psychology: Current perspectives.* New York: McGraw-Hill.

Bowman, S. (1994). *When the eagle screams: America's vulnerability to terrorism.* New York: Birch Lane Press.

Brockner, J. & Rubin, J. (1985). *The social psychology of conflict escalation and entrapment.* New York: Springer-Verlag.

Brookmeyer, R., Blades, N., Hugh-Jones, M., & Henderson, D. (2001). The statistical analysis of truncated data: Application to the Sverdlosk anthrax outbreak. *Biostatistics, 2,* 233-247.

Chemical and biological weapons threat: The urgent need for remedies, 101st Cong., Sess. 1 (1989a) (Statement of Claiborne Pell).

Chemical and biological weapons threat: The urgent need for remedies, 101st Cong., Sess. 1 (1989b) (Testimony of Judge Webster).

Clarke, B. G. (1993). Conflict termination: A rational model. *Terrorism, 16,* 25-50.

Combating terrorism: Federal response to a biological weapons attack, 107th Cong., 2nd Sess. (1991).

Combined News Service (1988, August 2). U.N. says Iraq used chemicals. *The Honolulu Advertiser,* pp. A1, A4.

Crenshaw, M. (1992). Current research on terrorism: The academic perspective. *Studies in Conflict and Terrorism, 15,* 1-11.

Department of Defense (1990a). *Hussein.* Available at: http://www.fas.org/irp/gulf/intel/950825/53240051_91r.txt

Department of Defense (1990b). *IZ chemical and biological warhead threat.* Available at: http://www.fas.org/irp/gulf/intel/961031/035pgv91d.txt

Department of Defense (1990c, August). *Views on Iraqi chemical warfare.* Available at: http://www.fas.org/irp/gulf/intel/961031/68320747.90.txt

Department of Defense (1990d, October). *Iraqi biological warfare (bw) developments.* Available at: http://www.fas.org/irp/gulf/intel/950825/011045di.90.txt

Department of Defense (1991a, April). *Reprisals against IZ civilians.* Available at: http://www/fas.org/irp/gulf/intel/950825/23403244_91r.txt

Department of Defense (1991b). *Iraqi chemical warfare.* Available at: http://www.globalsecurity.org/wmd/library/news/iraq/gulflink/intel/950727/23400353_91r.txt

Department of Justice (2001). *Use and management of criminal history record information: A comprehensive report.* Available at: http://www.ojp.usdoj.gov/bjs/pubalp2.htm#umchri.

DiGiovanni, C. (1999). Domestic terrorism with chemical or biological agents: Psychiatric aspects. *American Journal of Psychiatry, 156,* 1500-1505.

Douglass, J. (1995, November 2). Chemical and biological warfare unmasked. *The Wall Street Journal,* p. 2.

Federation of American Scientists, Working Group on Biological Weapons Verification (April, 1996). *Report of the subgroup on investigation of alleged use or release of biological toxin weapons agents.* Washington, DC: Author.

Gorman, S. (2002). Profiling terrorists. *National Journal, 34,* 1058.

Hagopian, M. (1978). *Regimes, movements, and ideologies.* New York: Longman.

Hall, H. V. (1996). Overview of lethal violence. In H. V. Hall (Ed.), *Lethal violence 2000: A sourcebook on fatal domestic, acquaintance and stranger aggression* (pp.1-51). Kamuela, HI: Pacific Institute for the Study of Conflict and Aggression.

Harff, B. & Gurr, T. R. (1989). Victims of the state: Genocides, politicides and group repression since 1945. *International Review of Victimology, 1,* 23-41.

Henry L. Stimson Center (1996, March). *First anniversary of Tokyo subway poison gas attack: Is the U.S. prepared for a similar attack?* (News Advisory). Washington, DC: Author.

Holsti, O. R. (1989). Crisis decision making. In P. E. Tetlock, J. L. Husbands, R. Jervis, P. C. Stern, & C. Tilly (Eds.), *Behavior, society, and nuclear war* (pp. 92-103). New York: Oxford University Press.

Hopple, G. W. (1993). Indications and warning and intelligence lessons. In B. W. Watson, B. George, P. Tsouras, & B. L. Cyr (Eds.), *Military lessons of the Gulf War* (pp. 146-156). London: Greenhill Books.

Horowitz, D. L. (1985). *Ethnic groups in conflict.* Los Angeles: University of California Press.

Hudson, R. A. (1999). *The sociology and psychology of terrorism: Who becomes a terrorist and why.* Washington, DC: Library of Congress.

Hughes, C. (1988, April 6). Iran parades survivors of poison gas before the media in New York hospital. *Honolulu Star-Bulletin,* p. A1.

Interview with Rick Atkinson (1996, August 5). *Frontline* [Television Series]. New York: WGBH Educational Foundation.

Iraq said to be setting up germ warfare production (1989, January 18). *Los Angeles Times,* p. A8.

Iraq warns: If attacked, we'll wreck half of Israel (1990, April 2). *Star Bulletin News Services*, p. A1.

Is military research hazardous to veterans' health? Lessons spanning half a century, 103th Cong., 2nd Session (1994).

Johnson, L. C. (2001). The future of terrorism. *American Behavioral Scientist, 44*, 894-913.

Kaplan, D. E. & Marshall, A. (1996). *The cult at the end of the world*. New York: Crown.

Kellen, K. (1979). *Terrorists–What are they like?* (Report No. N-1300-SL). Washington, DC: RAND Corporation.

Kellman, B. (2002). An international criminal law approach to bioterrorism. *Harvard Journal of Law and Public Policy, 25*, 721-743.

Leng, R. J. (1994). Interstate crisis escalation and war. In M. Potegal & J. F. Knutson (Eds.), *The dynamics of aggression* (pp. 307-332). Mahwah, NJ: Lawrence Erlbaum.

Leng, R. J. & Singer, J. D. (1988). Militarized interstate crises: The BCOW typology and its applications. *International Studies Quarterly, 32*, 155-173.

Lifton, R. J. (1976). *The life of the self*. New York: Simon and Schuster.

Lifton, R. J. (1982). *Death in life: Survivors of Hiroshima*. New York: Random House.

Lifton, R. J. & Falk, R. (1982). *Indefensible weapons: The political and psychological case against nuclearism*. New York: Basic Books.

Lifton, R. J. & Markusen, E. (1990). *The genocidal mentality: Nazi holocaust and nuclear threat*. New York: Basic Books.

Mackenzie, D. (2002). The insider: After months of bungled investigation, it now looks certain that America's anthrax attacks came from within. *New Scientist, 173*, 8.

Maerdian, F. R. (1930). The use of chemical warfare agents in civilian disturbances. *Chemical Warfare, 16*, 691-693.

Margolin, J. (1977). Psychological perspectives in terrorism. In Y. Alexander & S. M. Finger (Eds.), *Terrorism: Interdisciplinary perspectives* (pp. 271-277). New York: John Jay Press.

Mayer, J. D. (1993). The emotional madness of the dangerous leader. *Journal of Psychohistory, 20*, 331-348.

McCain, J. S. (1989). Proliferation in the 1990's: Implications for U.S. policy and force planning. *Strategic Review, 17*(3), 9-20.

McNitt, A. (1995). Government coercion: An exploratory analysis. *Social Sciences Journal, 32*, 195-205.

Mengel, R. W. (1979). Terrorism and new technologies of destruction: An overview of the potential risk. In A. Norton & M. Greenberg (Eds.), *Studies in nuclear terrorism* (pp. 27-52). Boston: GK Hall & Co.

Paltin, D. M. (1990). *The effects of nuclear holocaust imagery on self-concept*. Unpublished doctoral dissertation, United States International University, San Diego, CA.

Post, J. M. (1990). Current understanding of terrorist motivation and psychology: Implications for a differentiated antiterrorist policy. *Terrorism, 13*, 65-71.

Roberts, B. (1987). *Chemical warfare policy: Beyond the binary production decision* (Report No. IX, no. 3). Washington, DC: Center for Strategic and International Studies.

Robinson, J. P. (1991). Chemical weapons proliferation: The problem in perspective. In T. Findlay (Ed.), *Chemical weapons and missile proliferation* (pp. 19-35). Boulder, CO: Lynne Rienner.

Roux, G. (1992). *Ancient Iraq*. New York: Penguin Books.

Shultz, R. H. & Schmauder, J. M. (1994). Emerging regional conflicts and U.S. interests: Challenges and responses in the 1990s. *Studies in Conflict and Terrorism, 17,* 1-22.

Simon, J. D. (1989). *Terrorists and the potential use of biological weapons* (Report No. R-3771- AFMIC). Washington, DC: RAND Corporation.

Spiers, E. M. (1994). *Chemical and biological weapons: A study of proliferation.* New York: St. Martin's Press.

Stewart, J. & Zimmerman, L. J. (1989). To dehumanize and slaughter: A natural history model of massacres. *Great Plains Sociologist, 2,* 1-15.

Stohl, M. (1984). International dimensions of state terrorism. In M. Stohl & G. A. Lopez (Eds.), *The state as terrorist: The dynamics of governmental violence and repression* (pp. 5-12). Westport, CT: Greenwood Press.

The Anser Institute for Homeland Security (2002). *Darkwinter bioterrorism exercise.* Available at: http://www.homelandsecurity.org/darkwinter/index.cfm

Timmerman, K. R. (1991). *The death lobby*. Boston: Houghton Mifflin.

U.N. says Iraq used chemicals (1988, August 2). *Honolulu Advertiser*, p. A1.

United Nations (1969, July). *Report of the Secretary-General on chemical and bacteriological (biological)* (Report No. A/7575). Washington, DC: Author.

Watson, B. W., George, B., Tsouras, P., & Cyr, B. L. (Eds.) (1993). *Military lessons of the Gulf War*. London: Greenhill Books.

Wilson, M. A. (2000). Toward a model of terrorist behavior in hostage-taking incidents. *Journal of Conflict Resolution, 44,* 403-424.

Negotiating Crises:
The Evolution of Hostage/
Barricade Crisis Negotiation

John A. Call

SUMMARY. Over the last 25 to 30 years there has been significant growth in the knowledge base regarding how best to negotiate hostage/barricade crisis incidents. The goal of the present article is to review this evolution. More specifically, this article examines the multiple ways a crisis incident can be classified, analyzes the results of hostage/barricade incident databases, discusses different negotiation techniques and methods of negotiation analyses, and, finally, explores the impact of being taken captive on the victim. *[Article copies available for a fee from The Haworth Document Delivery Service: 1-800-HAWORTH. E-mail address: <docdelivery@haworthpress.com> Website: <http://www.HaworthPress.com> © 2003 by The Haworth Press, Inc. All rights reserved.]*

KEYWORDS. Hostage negotiation, barricade incidents, terrorism, crisis negotiation

---

John A. Call, PhD, JD, is affiliated with Crisis Management Consultants, Inc.

Address correspondence to: John A. Call, PhD, JD, Crisis Management Consultants, Inc., 5100 North Brookline, Suite 700, Oklahoma City, OK 73112 (E-mail: cmc@crisisinc.com).

[Haworth co-indexing entry note]: "Negotiating Crises: The Evolution of Hostage/Barricade Crisis Negotiation." Call, John A. Co-published simultaneously in *Journal of Threat Assessment* (The Haworth Press, Inc.) Vol. 2, No. 3, 2003, pp. 69-94; and: *Terrorism: Strategies for Intervention* (ed: Harold V. Hall) The Haworth Press, Inc., 2003, pp. 69-94. Single or multiple copies of this article are available for a fee from The Haworth Document Delivery Service [1-800-HAWORTH, 9:00 a.m. - 5:00 p.m. (EST). E-mail address: docdelivery@haworthpress.com].

The act of unlawfully taking and holding a person against his or her will is, unfortunately, an all too frequent human activity and one that has a history as old as humankind. One of the earliest descriptions of the use of a special weapons and tactical (SWAT) team to recover hostage victims is in the book of Genesis, Chapter 14. Abraham's nephew, Lot, amongst others, was taken captive by the King of Elam. Upon hearing of this disaster, Abraham immediately gathered from his own household a band of 318 specially trained and armed men and together they pursued the king, overtaking him near the springs of the Jordan. Abraham's men and allies attacked and routed the king and his army, and pursued those who remained almost as far as Damascus. The pursuers then returned to their homeland, bringing back all of the spoils and captives that had been carried away.

Abraham's use of the tactical option has been relied upon through the ages as perhaps the most common method of handling such crises. Negotiating with the captor has been another, though less frequently used, technique. An early example of this procedure can be found in Greek mythology. Hades, king of the underworld, kidnapped Persephone, who was daughter of the goddess Demeter. In her anger, Demeter caused all the crops on Earth to die. To prevent the destruction of Earth's inhabitants, Zeus sent Eros as his "negotiator" to confer with Hades in an attempt to resolve the crisis. Following these negotiations, Hades agreed to let Persephone return to Earth during the spring of each year. In return, Demeter permitted Earth's crops to grow during Persephone's visits but then caused them to die in the fall when her daughter returned to the underworld.

Not only is this myth perhaps the first recorded use of crisis negotiation, but its conclusion may also be the first documented example of the Stockholm Syndrome (Rahe, Karson, Howard, Rubin, & Poland, 1990). The legend concludes that Persephone, although at first terrified of Hades, later fell in love and married him. This paradoxical response to captivity was more recently observed in 1973 when a female hostage divorced her husband to marry a bank robber who had held her and three others captive for 131 hours in the vault of the Sveriges Kreditbank in Stockholm, Sweden (Strentz, 1980).

The idea of negotiating with a captor, although not new, did not receive much modern commentary until after 1972. During the mid-1960s, the concern of law enforcement focused on how best to respond to criminals with more lethal and sophisticated weapons, as well as how to deal with societal unrest and terrorist incidents. The answer, it was believed, lay in employing paramilitary special weapons and tactical

(SWAT) teams, analogous to Abraham's 318 specially trained and armed men. In 1967, the Los Angeles Police Department became the first to implement SWAT teams. Thus, by the early 1970s, there were three options for responding to hostage or barricade incidents: (1) the first officer on the scene talked the perpetrator into giving up; (2) law enforcement walked away from the incident; or (3) the police used force (Hatcher, Mohandie, Turner, & Gelles, 1998).

There have been problems with these various options, however. For example, in October 1971, during a hijacked airliner incident, the Federal Bureau of Investigation (FBI) decided to use the tactical option. The episode concluded in the death of two hostages and a perpetrator. In subsequent litigation, the U. S. Court of Appeals for the 6th Circuit chastised the FBI's inept handling of the crisis incident, finding that the bureau had turned "what had been a successful 'waiting game', during which two persons safely left the plane, into a 'shooting match' that left three persons dead" (*Downs vs. U.S.*, 1975, p. 1002; Higginbotham, 1994).

In March of 1972, Palestinian terrorists took eleven Israeli Olympic athletes hostage in Munich, Germany. At the conclusion of that standoff, 22 people were dead, including a policeman, 10 terrorists, and all of the hostages (Soskis & Van Zandt, 1986). This incident came to be known as the "Munich Massacre."

Because of these and similar hostage/barricade incidents, law enforcement policy analysts began to rethink the need for alternatives to the tactical option. Accordingly, various metropolitan police agencies, and eventually the FBI, designed and implemented hostage recovery programs. In 1973, the New York City Police Department initiated a program that not only included SWAT teams but also detectives trained as negotiators (Bolz & Hershey, 1979; Schlossberg, 1980). Following New York City's lead, the FBI likewise developed a similar program (Soskis & Van Zandt, 1986).

Since the pioneering work of Schlossberg (1980) and Bolz (Bolz & Hershey, 1979), the use of trained crisis negotiators has steadily increased in law enforcement agencies throughout the United States. Butler, Leitenberg and Fuselier (1993) reported that of those law enforcement agencies responding to their survey, 68% of state police agencies ($n = 17$), 96% of the large municipal agencies ($n = 125$), and 30% of the small municipal law enforcement agencies ($n = 158$) indicated that they had a designated hostage negotiator. Bahn and Louden (1999) found that most of these specialists worked only part-time as negotiators

(94%), were deployed on average about 11 times a year, and received approximately 32 hours of in-service training per year.

Over the last quarter century there has been significant growth in the knowledge base regarding crisis incidents and how best to handle them. The act of capturing and holding a person against his or her will is now better understood in that it is recognized that various motives can spur these events. Not all crisis incidents necessarily consist of hostage situations. There has been an evolution in how negotiators identify and fulfill their role. More specifically, the first generation of specialists primarily saw themselves as "hostage" negotiators; however, the present generation now perceive themselves as "crisis" negotiators. This change in self-perception is due, in significant part, to a growing understanding of the similarities and differences between hostage and barricade situations. The goal of the present article is to review this evolution.

TYPOLOGY ANALYSES

A primary goal of crisis negotiations is to resolve a standoff with as little loss of life as possible. In order to accomplish this goal, the negotiator must interact with the perpetrator by using normative bargaining techniques (Donohue, Ramesh, Kaufmann, & Smith, 1991). The starting point of the process, however, resides in classifying the incident because the key question in any crisis incident is whether or not there exists a bargaining range. Depending upon the classification or typology of the crisis incident, there may be some bargaining ability on the part of the negotiator.

By definition, a traditional hostage situation occurs when one hostage taker or more holds one or more hostage and threatens harm to the latter, unless a third party fulfills the demands of the former. Thus, hostage taking can be defined as a triadic event–an event that involves three participants (Soskis & Van Zandt, 1986; Call, 1996).

Hostage situations are analogous to theater, albeit a theater of terror rather than amusement. The hostage taker is the star, the hostages the supporting cast, and law enforcement and the public the audience. Since the hostage taker wants something from a third party, there is a significant chance that a bargaining range can be found. Hostage situations are characterized by the following: (1) the hostage taker is more or less goal oriented; (2) the hostage taker makes substantive demands, usually including escape; (3) the hostage taker needs police to facilitate demands, (4) the hostage taker's primary motivation is having the demands met;

and (5) the hostage taker realizes that keeping some hostages alive prevents a tactical response.

However, other crisis incidents involving captors and captives occur and are best termed *barricade-victim incidents*. From the perpetrator's point of view, barricade incidents are dyadic, rather than triadic, events in that they are occurrences involving only the perpetrator and the victim. Furthermore, instead of being analogous to theater, these crisis situations are more akin to secret rituals. The captor is the avenging priest and the victim the sacrifice.

In the barricade-victim situation, the victim is not a hostage in the traditional sense. Rather, the captor holds the victim for an expressive, rather than instrumental, purpose. Instrumental hostage taking occurs when the hostage taker is attempting to achieve a goal or change some aspect of society. Expressive victim taking is motivated by internal emotions and impulses that are often quite personal and obscure (Miron & Goldstein, 1979). In particular, there are no substantive demands made upon a third party by the perpetrator. In fact, the perpetrator wants nothing from a third party.

A classic example of the barricade-victim incident is when a man who holds his ex-wife at gunpoint, lets his children out of the barricaded house, shoots his ex-wife, and commits suicide. The victim in this example is actually a "homicide-to-be" rather than a hostage (Fuselier, Van Zandt, & Lanceley, 1991). Since the captor has what he or she wants (i.e., the victim), a bargaining range is often unattainable. Characteristics of the non-hostage barricade-victim situation include the following: (1) no clear goal; (2) no substantive demands from the perpetrator; (3) an absence of rational thinking; (4) the focus is directed against the person held; and (5) expressive, emotional, and senseless ventilation is prominently displayed by the perpetrator.

In a third type of crisis situation, there is no identified victim. Rather, the perpetrator is armed and barricaded and the authorities attempt to talk him or her into surrendering. Examples are a trapped criminal who is barricaded in a convenience store or a mentally ill person who is suicidal, armed, and barricaded in his or her home. Depending upon the situation, a bargaining range may or may not be possible (see Table 1).

There are several other useful ways to profile crisis situations where crisis negotiation techniques are used. One is to classify the situation as to whether or not the location of the victim and perpetrator is known and contained (a siege) or whether the location is not known and thus not contained (a non-siege; Lanceley, 1999; see Table 2).

TABLE 1. Crisis Incident Typologies

Type	Interaction	Description
Hostage Situation	Perpetrator-Hostage-Third Person(s)	Hostage taker makes substantive demands (usually instrumental, some may be expressive) of a third party threatening harm to hostages if the demands are not met.
Barricade-Victim	Perpetrator-Victim	Perpetrator does not make substantive demands of a third party. Any demands made are typically non-substantive in nature.
Barricade-No Victim	Perpetrator	Perpetrator may or may not make demands and may or may not be willing to bargain.

TABLE 2. Victim Location vs. Perpetrator Demands

Demands	Location	
	Known (Siege)	Unknown (Non-Siege)
Substantive	Bargaining control probably exists.	Bargaining control possibly exists.
Non-Substantive	Bargaining control possibly exists.	Bargaining control probably does not exist.

Depending upon this type of crisis there may exist greater or lesser bargaining ability on the part of the law enforcement negotiator. For example, in a situation where the victim has been kidnapped, the location of the victim and perpetrator is not known, and there are no demands being made of a third party, there is no bargaining control and there is little, if anything, a crisis negotiator can do.

On the other end of the continuum, however, when the perpetrator has kidnapped a victim, the victim and perpetrator are contained within a known perimeter under the control of the authorities, and the perpetrator is making substantive demands, there exists bargaining control on the part of the negotiator.

A more detailed way of analyzing the *siege* subtype of crisis situation is described in Table 3 in that there are three subtypes: (1) the deliberate siege; (2) the spontaneous siege; and (3) the anticipated siege. An example of a deliberate siege is a barricade-victim situation involving a jilted male lover and a woman who is a "homicide-to-be." A spontaneous siege is exemplified by a trapped criminal, with or without hostages. Finally, an example of an anticipated siege is a group of religious fanatics who are collecting illegal weapons and explosives in their compound, such as occurred with the Branch Davidians in Waco, Texas.

The key for the crisis negotiator is to determine the reason for the siege and determine the nature of the demands being made by the perpetrator (i.e., instrumental vs. expressive; substantive vs. non-substantive). Depending upon the correct analyses of these two factors, the crisis negotiator may or may not have bargaining power.

As observed in the above discussion, analyzing the perpetrator's demand type is crucial. In fact, analyzing the types of demands being made by the perpetrator is another way of understanding and classifying a crisis incident (see Table 4). There are instrumental demands, expressive demands, substantive demands, and non-substantive demands. Basically, the crisis negotiator has bargaining power only if the perpetrator

TABLE 3. Siege Typologies

General Category	Description
Deliberate	Perpetrator deliberately initiates the siege situation—wanting to provoke a response from the authorities. Depending upon other factors, i.e., whether or not the incident is a Hostage Situation or a Barricade-Victim situation, substantive demands may or may not be made.
Spontaneous	Perpetrator inadvertently precipitates the siege situation. Hostages/victims may or may not be present. Substantive demands may or may not be made.
Anticipated	Perpetrator expected that at sometime or another the authorities would seek his or her arrest. Substantive demands are usually not made in a Barricade-No Victim situation. Substantive demands may or may not be made if the siege is also a Hostage Situation.

TABLE 4. Demand Typologies

General Category	Description
Instrumental	Demand characteristics best described as "objective," e.g., money, transportation, food, liquor, drugs.
Expressive	Demand characteristics best described as "subjective," e.g., perpetrator wants to talk to family member, perpetrator wants to make a statement to the media regarding delusional beliefs.
Substantive	Victims are threatened to obtain concessions from a third party; the demands may be instrumental or expressive.
Non-Substantive	Demands are not made, or, if they are, they are trivial and not related to the reason(s) the victim(s) are threatened.

makes substantive demands, which may be either instrumental or expressive. Anecdotal reports suggest that one sign of imminent lethality is the determination that the perpetrator is not demanding anything from a third party to release the hostage/victim (Fuselier, Van Zandt, & Lanceley, 1991).

Finally, one last way the crisis negotiator can classify the crisis situation is based on a hostage taker typology (Call, 1996; see Table 5). Six types of hostage takers are noted: (1) emotionally disturbed; (2) political extremists; (3) religious fanatics; (4) criminals; (5) prison inmates; and (6) a combination of two or more of the others. There are also multiple subtypes, as the following review by Call (1996) reveals:

> Starting first with the Emotionally Disturbed category, Fuselier (1988), following Strentz (1986), noted four subtypes. These are (a) paranoid, various types, (b) depressed, various types, (c) inadequate personality, and (d) antisocial personality. The use of the latter subtype is questionable in the context of the emotionally disturbed category. This subtype is descriptive of a personality disorder, not an emotional disorder. Logically, it is much more likely that individuals with this personality disorder will be involved in hostage incidents with instrumental motivations, such as a trapped criminal or terrorist skyjacking, rather than the expressive acts of the emotionally disabled.

Likewise, the concept of inadequate personality is believed to be of limited value as a subtype. Inadequate personality disorder is no longer a diagnostic category as noted in the Diagnostic and Statistical Manual of Mental Disorders, Fourth Edition (American Psychiatric Association, 1994). . . .

In his analysis of the emotionally disturbed category of hostage taker, Pearce (1977) described the following subtypes: (a) the brain damaged individual, (b) the elderly/senile individual, (c) the retarded, depressed person, (d) the agitated, depressed person, (e) the schizophrenic, and (f) the barricaded person as an equivalent to attempted suicide (suicide by cop). . . .

Kennedy and Dyer (1992), discussing a small sample of men who took their own children hostage, noted that each had a history of alcohol abuse, drug abuse, or both, and a family history and ethos of violent and unstable relationships. The hostage taking was initiated by situational stress within the family. A similar phenomenon was reported by Gist and Perry (1985). . . .

With respect to the Political Extremist, Knutson (1980) described two subtypes: the reluctant captor and the deliberate hostage taker. Her research suggested that the majority of American politically motivated hostage takers, at least until 1980, can be classified as the former subtype. Her interviews with these individuals indicated that they were unwilling, if not unable, to kill their hostages. . . . Knutson summed up their personality style as dreamers and philosophers whose violent act was part of an attempt to right a wrong or a perceived injustice.

Deliberate hostage takers, on the other hand, are perfectly willing to execute their captives. The hostages are discardable implements to be used as long as needed by the hostage taker. They are supremely goal oriented but unfeeling, like a shark seeking a meal. Although uncaring, they are well aware of the hostages' emotions but use them to their own ends. They will terrorize one minute and act friendly the next in their effort to control the situation. . . . Interestingly, Knutson found in her sample that, as children, both subtypes of hostage takers were likely to have experienced a close brush with death.

There have been other attempts to explain the political extremist from a psychological point of view. Ferracuti (1982) concluded that the best approach to understanding these individuals is to use what he terms "the subcultural theory." In simple terms, political extremists live in their own sealed communities or subcultures with their own unique self-imposed value systems. What may be relevant for the culture at large may be meaningless for the political extremist's subculture and vice versa. To understand a particular subtype of political extremist, one must first understand the values and mores of that subculture. Global theories applicable to all political extremists may be unobtainable. Thorough understanding may come only via investigation of each subculture. . . .

[Cooper (1981) first enumerated the general hostage taker category of the Religious Fanatic.] With respect to understanding possible subtypes of this category, the advice of Ferracuti (1982) concerning understanding political extremists probably applies. A thorough understanding of religious fanatics will likely require analysis of a particular cult's internal mores and values.

The Criminal category is usually thought of as consisting of the trapped criminal. For example, the bank robber who is unable to make his escape before the police arrive. . . . The major subtype in the criminal category is the criminal psychopath. The criminal psychopath is also believed to be a major subtype in the Prison category of hostage taker. However, other subtypes also occur. For example, in the November 23, 1987 Oakdale, Louisiana, riot where 200 Cuban inmates held 26 people hostage at a Federal Detention Center, the only hostage seriously physically injured was stabbed by an emotionally disturbed inmate. This occurrence is also an example of a Combination hostage taker (Call, 1996, pp. 564-567).

Depending upon the type and subtype of hostage taker with which the negotiator is dealing, experience dictates the use of certain negotiation strategies. For example, Lanceley (1999) makes the following suggestions when negotiating with an individual who has been diagnosed with schizophrenia: (1) avoid the use of family members, since they may be a part of the delusional system; (2) do not try to talk the perpetrator out of his or her delusional system; (3) let the perpetrator discuss concerns; and (4) if one of the demands of the perpetrator is media attention, this demand may be a negotiable item.

DATABASE ANALYSES

Call (1996) noted that there had been no ongoing nationwide collection of information on hostage incidents; however, this situation no longer persists. Following the death of 96 Branch Davidians in Waco, Texas on April 19, 1993, then U. S. Attorney General Janet Reno di-

TABLE 5. Hostage Taker Typologies

General Category	Possible Subtypes
Emotionally Disturbed	1. Brain Damaged 2. Elderly/Senile 3. Depressed, Various Types 4. Paranoid, Various Types 5. Schizophrenic 6. Substance Abuser 7. Family Disputes
Political Extremists	1. Reluctant Captors 2. Deliberate Hostage Takers
Religious Fanatics	
Criminals	1. Antisocial Personality Disorder/Trapped Criminal 2. Antisocial Personality Disorder/Kidnapper
Prison Inmates	Antisocial Personality Disorder
Combination	

Note. From: Call, J. A. (1996). The hostage triad: Takers, victims, and negotiators. In H. V. Hall (Ed.), *Lethal violence 2000: A sourcebook on fatal domestic, acquaintance and stranger aggression* (pp. 561-588). Kamuela, HI: Pacific Institute for the Study of Conflict and Aggression. Copyright 1996 by Pacific Institute for the Study of Conflict and Aggression. Reprinted with permission.

rected the FBI to develop a nationwide hostage incident database. Three years later, just eight days before the anniversary of the Waco tragedy, the Hostage/Barricade Report (HoBaS) was disseminated by the FBI to local law enforcement agencies, which is a hostage and barricade incident data-collecting questionnaire. Whenever a hostage incident occurs, the responding law enforcement agency is requested to complete the HoBaS questionnaire and forward it to the FBI. The HoBaS questionnaire seeks information regarding: (1) the incident; (2) nature of contacts made by law enforcement during the incident; (3) resolution of the incident; (4) post-incident information; (5) ancillary information regarding negotiator and SWAT interaction and training; (6) subject data; and (7) hostage/victim data.

Prior to the development of HoBaS, only a small sample of relevant databases existed in the public domain. Fortunately, behavioral scientists have continued to research this area (Feldmann, 1998), since public access to HoBaS is difficult. The information in these unrestricted databases is enlightening. However, when analyzing this information one must keep in mind the definitional structure of the data as well as the time frame during which the data was collected.

In the 1970s, Mickolus (1976), who later became a Central Intelligence Agency analyst, developed a computerized database of 3,329 international terrorist incidents from 1968 through 1977 while he was a graduate student at Yale. These incidents occurred outside the United States. Mickolus named this database "International Terrorism: Attributes of Terrorist Events" or ITERATE.

Head (1990) was one of the first to thoroughly analyze this database and report his conclusions in the public domain. He was particularly interested in the ITERATE data which included political extremist hostage-taking incidents. Head divided the ITERATE database into three subcategories: hijacking, kidnapping, and barricade incidents. He found that from 1968 through 1977 hostage takers usually worked in groups of three or more and that hostage incidents were not particularly lethal (in 17% of incidents, hostages were wounded and in 19% of incidents, there were one or more deaths). Barricade incidents were the most lethal, with explosives the most common means of death. When negotiators were used, incidents were less lethal.

Friedland and Merari (1992) developed a database of 69 international and domestic political extremist hostage-taking incidents between the years of 1979 and 1988. These incidents were ether a barricade situation or a hijacking of transport. These researchers found that there were usually five or fewer hostage takers (63.3%), the majority of hostages were civilian (59.4%), the average number of hostages in a barricade incident was 35, the average number of hostages in a hijacking was 131, the majority of incidents lasted 24 hours or less (43.8%), and the most common outcome was violent (31.1%). A violent conclusion to the incident was more probable if it was a barricade situation, a trained rescue team was present, and no attempts at negotiation were made.

No other recent databases regarding political extremist hostage taking have been published. However, in analyzing the data from the ITERATE database from 1968 through the Friedland and Merari (1992) database until 1988, there appears to be a trend toward political extremist hostage taking becoming more lethal (19% vs. 31.1%). Furthermore, this trend may well be continuing. Anecdotal review of more recent political extremist activity suggests that terrorists appear more prone to kill their captives rather than negotiate. For example, in the United States on September 11, 2001, 239 people were taken temporary hostage by Arab terrorists in four airplane hijackings. Initially, this event may seem comparable to the dramatic capture of four planes over a three-day period by Arab terrorists, almost exactly 31 years earlier, in September 1970. However, the unfortunate difference is that in 1970 the terrorists landed the four planes and eventually released the hostages, whereas in 2001 terrorists deliberately killed all the passengers and never attempted to negotiate.

Practically speaking, the data suggest that most American law enforcement negotiators do not deal with political extremist hostage or barricade incidents. Head (1990) developed and analyzed two other databases in his research efforts. One database, the Hostage Event Analytic Database (HEAD), contained 3,330 incidents of domestic hostage taking which occurred between 1973 and 1982. The majority of the hostage takers fit the criminal or prison inmate (52%) or emotionally disturbed (18%) typologies; the majority of hostage takers were young (25% below age 30), white (61%), male (80%), and acted alone; the typical number of hostages was one (47%) or two (15%); the most common location of the incident was a home (20%); the most common weapon used was a handgun (31%); the typical incident duration was less than one day (31% ended within 6 hours); the majority of incidents were non-lethal (87%); and a negotiator was usually used during the crisis event (64%).

A third database analyzed by Head (1990) was comprised of 137 hostage incidents handled by members of the New York Police Department Hostage Recovery Program from 1973 through 1982. Once again, the most common type of hostage taker was criminal or prison inmate (58%) or emotionally disturbed (26%); the majority of hostage takers were young (46% below age of 30), white (35%), male (87%), and acted alone; the typical number of hostages was one (43%) or two (26%); the most frequent incident location was a home (41%); the most common weapon was a handgun (41%); the typical incident duration was less than one day (61% ended within 6 hours); and the majority of incidents were non-lethal (91%).

Butler et al. (1993) developed a database of 410 hostage incidents that occurred between 1986 and 1988. Of note is the fact that all of these incidents were reported by law enforcement agencies employing negotiators. These researchers found the most frequent hostage taker typology to be emotionally disturbed (71% in large police departments and 88% in small police departments) and the next most frequent was criminal (15% and 6% respectively); the majority of incidents were non-lethal (90%) and the most frequent outcome was a negotiated surrender (65%).

Feldmann (1998) began assembling a database of hostage/barricade incidents that occurred in Kentucky ($n = 120$ incidents). This database is an ongoing project and provides an excellent example of what researchers in every state should be doing. He identified six categories of hostage/barricade incidents in his sample: (1) personal or domestic disputes (31%); (2) subjects involved in criminal acts (26%); (3) mentally ill persons for whom no other motivation was present (19%); (4) incidents associated with workplace violence (12%); (5) alcohol or drug related incidents (8%); and (6) incidents involving students and schools (5%).

Data analyses by Feldmann (1998) revealed certain characteristics common to all categories and certain characteristics unique to each category. General characteristics that he observed were:

1. the acts were usually committed by males under the age of 30;
2. offenders most often acted alone;
3. the perpetrator frequently had a prior criminal record;
4. offenders were most often motivated by an interpersonal dispute or grievance, complicated by an underlying psychiatric disorder;
5. firearms were implicated in nearly three-fourths of the incidents;
6. most incidents resulted in injury or death to either some of the hostages or to the perpetrator (87.5% of cases);
7. nearly all of the offenders had psychiatric diagnoses, regardless of the category to which they belonged;
8. personality disorders, substance abuse disorders, and mood disorders comprised the largest diagnostic groups in the study;
9. the majority of incidents were associated with suicidal intent;
10. alcohol and drug use were relatively common among subjects, either in the form of acute intoxication or a history of abuse;
11. warning signs prior to the incident were apparent in over 60% of the cases, but were infrequently recognized or reported;
12. a majority of incidents were negotiated, but negotiations were successful less than 40% of the time;
13. SWAT teams were deployed in over two-thirds of cases, and an assault was carried out in slightly less than 40% of incidents (Feldman, 1998, pp. 15-16).

Unique characteristics that Feldman observed in the personal/domestic category were: (1) hostage takers were primarily white males in their late 20s and early 30s; (2) perpetrators demonstrated greatest risk of suicide compared to other categories; (3) the incident most often occurred in a home; (4) clear warning signs (threats or harassment of victim) were present (80% of cases); (5) victim was current or former spouse, girlfriend, or child; (6) victim was stalked in 66% of cases before the incident occurred; (7) negotiations were successful in only 30% of cases; and (8) injuries or deaths occurred in 95% of cases.

The unique characteristics that Feldman observed in the criminal category were: (1) perpetrators were primarily African-American males with a mean age of 24 years; (2) perpetrators were most often engaged in robbery attempts (74%); (3) negotiations were successful in 68% of cases; and (4) injuries or death occurred in 45% of cases.

Distinctive characteristics Feldman noted in the mentally ill category were: (1) most perpetrators were in their mid-30s; (2) most common incident location was a public place such as a mall or government building; (3) a wide variety of weapons were used, not just handguns; (4) high incidence of barricade situations without hostages; (5) demands were bizarre or nonexistent; (6) resolution most frequently a tactical assault; and (7) relatively low injury or fatality rate.

The distinctive characteristics Feldman observed in the workplace violence category were: (1) perpetrators were older individuals, usually in their mid-40s; (2) 50% had served in the military; (3) over 60% had an excessive interest in weapons; (4) prior warning signs and stalking were common; (5) there was a very high likelihood of injury or death; (6) very high likelihood of suicide; and (7) very low likelihood of negotiation success.

As noted earlier, substance abuse was common in all six categories. However, the alcohol and drug related category was classified as one wherein the perpetrator either was attempting to obtain substances or was under the effects of acute intoxication as the only motivation for the incident. Unique factors observed in this category were: (1) handguns were frequently used; (2) injuries or deaths occurred quite early in the incident; (3) initiating negotiations was quite difficult; and (4) once negotiations had begun, however, there was a high rate of successful resolution.

Finally, the student category contained the following unique characteristics: (1) the youngest perpetrators, with a mean age of 18; (2) the highest number of hostages, from 10 to 40; (3) the perpetrators carried multiple weapons; and (4) once negotiations had begun the rate of successful resolution was high.

The databases discussed above represent most, if not all, of the statistical research that exists in the public domain. Except for this database research the majority of the scientific investigation into crisis negotiation has been performed by law enforcement personnel and the few behavioral scientists that work with them. Likewise, most of this work is anecdotal and theoretical in nature. Almost no empirical research has been performed. Thus, much work remains for future investigators.

NEGOTIATION ANALYSES

Perpetrators involved in a hostage or barricade situation, even if the incident is planned or anticipated, are almost always in a state of autonomic nervous system hyper-arousal. Increasingly narrow and constricted thinking, decreased attention span, heightened emotionality, and a disorganized, shot-gun approach to problem solving characterize this crisis state. The initial tasks of the crisis negotiator are to: (1) establish rapport; (2) stall for time; and (3) gather information.

The key question facing the negotiator in any hostage/barricade situation is whether or not a bargaining range exists. In the true hostage situation, such a range can often be found. In a non-hostage situation, such as a barricade-victim incident, there is often little or no opportunity for bargaining control. Deciding what type of situation the negotiator faces determines whether he or she uses both crisis intervention and bargaining techniques or primarily crisis intervention techniques.

In true hostage situations, the hostage taker initially attempts to utilize a crisis bargaining style best defined as brinkmanship. Crisis bargaining, or brinkmanship, is characterized by: (1) the use of coercion; (2) bargaining for high stakes; (3) focusing on only one alternative; (4) the feeling of urgency; (5) high emotional content; (6) prevalence of face or ego issues; (7) lack of complete information; and (8) failure to work out detailed plans (Donohue, Ramesh, Kaufmann, & Smith, 1991). On the other hand, the negotiator attempts to move the hostage taker's bargaining style away from coercive brinkmanship to one of cooperative, normative bargaining. Normative bargaining is based upon the concept of *quid pro quo*. To do this, negotiators attempt to slow down the interaction, develop multiple options, avoid face issues, control emotions, and create information resources.

As a starting point, the negotiator must develop a relationship (Rogan, Donohue, & Lyles, 1990; Schlossberg, 1980). This is best conceptualized as a negotiation within a negotiation (Donohue & Roberto,

1993) and requires something more than urging the subject to "just trust me." Lanceley (1999) noted that "contrary to what some people might suppose, the primary skill of good negotiators is not smooth talking, but practiced listening" (p. 17). Therefore, after introducing oneself to the perpetrator and asking if anyone has medical needs, the negotiator uses active listening techniques to help build rapport. Active listening is defined as the ability to view a situation from another's perspective and to let that person know that one understands that perspective (see Table 6).

Active listening is also the primary tool of crisis intervention. Empirical research by Donohue and Roberto (1993) suggests that negotiators and perpetrators develop a relatively stable relational pattern fairly quickly in the negotiation process. Donohue et al. (1991) view the initial phases of hostage negotiation as consisting of five stages: (1) intelligence gathering; (2) introduction and relationship development; (3) problem clarification and relationship development; (4) problem solving; and (5) resolution. Later research has suggested that context plays an important role and no one model best describes how negotiations progress. In other words, negotiation may progress in a stage fashion, moving from crisis bargaining toward normative bargaining via phases, or negotiation progress may be interdependent with integrative and distributive bargaining intertwined. However, the negotiation may also remain fixed and separate, with the perpetrator remaining in crisis bargaining mode while the negotiator attempts to bargain normatively (Donohue & Roberto, 1996).

Also, negotiation success has been defined as the surrender of the perpetrator and release of the hostage/victims. Although this is an enviable goal, in some cases it may not be realistic. No longer does a tactical solution equate with a negotiation failure. Rather, negotiating success is judged by stabilizing an incident through "verbal containment," keeping law enforcement officers from making dangerous entries, buying time for intelligence gathering and resource arrival, and preventing further loss of life.

No matter what the ultimate outcome of the crisis incident, the negotiator is always responsible for developing and sharing with the on-site commander two key expert opinions: (1) the extent of negotiation progress and (2) an estimate of the likelihood of imminent lethality.

A review of the crisis negotiation literature reveals that there are eleven factors that indicate progress is being made in a crisis negotiation (Crisis Management Consultants, Inc., 2002; Fuselier & Romana, 1996; Fuselier & Van Zandt, 1987; Lanceley, 1999; Soskis & Van Zandt, 1986). These factors are:

TABLE 6. Active Listening Techniques

General Category	Description
Emotional Labeling	Negotiator labels and responds to perpetrator's emotions not just his or her statement content.
Paraphrasing	Negotiator summarizes perpetrator's statements.
Reflecting or Mirroring	Negotiator repeats the perpetrator's last word or phrase with a rising inflection suggesting a question.
Minimal Encouragers	Negotiator uses short questions to encourage further statements.
"I" Messages	Negotiator lets the perpetrator know how and why the negotiator is feeling a certain way and what the perpetrator can do to remedy the situation.
Open-Ended Questions	Negotiator asks questions that cannot be answered with a yes or no.
Silence	Negotiator responds with silence that, in context, encourages the perpetrator to make further statements.

1. there have been no additional injuries since negotiations have begun;
2. verbal and physical threats are decreasing;
3. conversation on the part of the perpetrator is increasing;
4. the perpetrator is making more personal statements;
5. the perpetrator is making fewer instrumental demands;
6. rapport is developing between the primary negotiator and the perpetrator;
7. the perpetrator is demonstrating lowered emotionality (via voice level, etc.) and increased rationality;
8. normative bargaining is increasing and crisis bargaining, or brinksmanship, is decreasing;
9. deadlines made by the perpetrator have passed with no further injuries;
10. some of the hostages have been released;
11. the perpetrator is discussing the surrender process.

Signs of imminent lethality include the following:

1. perpetrator has initiated a deliberate confrontation with the authorities and has made no attempt to escape;

2. the victim is known to the perpetrator and was selected by the perpetrator;
3. there is a history of problems between the victim and perpetrator;
4. perpetrator is not making any substantive demands;
5. perpetrator has a history of similar incidents;
6. perpetrator has suffered multiple recent stressors;
7. perpetrator perceives a loss of face and/or control;
8. perpetrator lacks social support systems;
9. additional injuries have occurred since the negotiation started;
10. threats against the hostage(s)/victim(s) are increasing;
11. perpetrator's emotionality is increasing and rationality is decreasing;
12. conversation is decreasing;
13. no rapport between negotiator and perpetrator;
14. perpetrator is making suicide threats or giving suicide clues (Crisis Management Consultants, Inc., 2002; Fuselier & Romana, 1996; Fuselier, Van Zandt, & Lanceley, 1991; Lanceley, 1999; Soskis & Van Zandt, 1986).

The above literature, while anecdotal in nature, is the result of many years of practical experience. Most of the authors are ex-FBI hostage negotiators and, at one time or another, worked closely with the FBI Hostage Rescue Team headquartered at the FBI Academy. However, it should be noted that the above negotiation progress factors, as well as the signs of imminent lethality, are not equally weighted in importance. Rather, these factors and signs are recommended as guideposts that, when taken in context with the totality of the crisis situation, help the negotiator develop an expert opinion as to progress and imminent threat of lethality.

Crisis negotiation is a team enterprise. An important maxim is that one never negotiates alone. At a minimum there should be a primary negotiator, a secondary negotiator, and a team leader. Depending on the circumstances, there may be more elaborate six-person teams staged in three shifts. Each shift would have a primary negotiator, secondary negotiator, negotiation team leader, tactical liaison, resource coordinator, and behavioral science consultant (Fuselier & Van Zandt, 1987; Lanceley, 1999).

Documentation of the negotiation process is critical. The secondary negotiator, or the recorder on larger teams, needs to record all negotiation events in order to reconstruct events for court testimony and, perhaps more importantly, to help acquire, categorize, and analyze perpetrator, victim, demand, and negotiation progress factors, thus focusing the negotiator and commander as to what is happening.

During the latter part of the 1990s, the FBI evaluated but did not implement a dedicated computer software program entitled the Personality Profile Module Computer Program (PPM). This ambitious program was designed, in part, to help negotiators keep track of negotiation events as they occurred. The program also included encrypted internet access to HoBaS data, threat assessment scales, subject and incident history forms, personality profile data, suggested negotiation and incident strategies, and report writing features.

Recently, another more user-friendly software program has been published; however, this one is in the public domain. The program is entitled "The Crisis Negotiator" and is comprised of 13 databases arranged in five modules: (1) Perpetrator/Victim Data; (2) Demands-Objectives-Assessment; (3) Lethality Assessment; (4) Negotiation Analyses; and (5) Action Guides. The Crisis Negotiator is designed to help systematize and understand perpetrator demands and negotiator objectives, measure and analyze negotiation progress, assess the potential for lethality, and, identify warning signs of imminent lethality on the part of the perpetrator (Crisis Management Consultants, Inc., 2002). Careful documentation and analysis is key for crisis negotiation success. Therefore, negotiation teams need to utilize dedicated software programs or keep detailed handwritten notes.

VICTIM ANALYSES

Being held against one's will and threatened with bodily harm and/or death is an obvious psychological trauma that has severe short- and long-term emotional and behavioral repercussions. Initially, the victim usually experiences the phenomenon of frozen fright (Fuselier, 1991; Symonds, 1980a, 1980b). The victim cannot flee because his or her freedom of movement is taken away. Thus, in fear, he or she focuses attention on the perpetrator. The hostage taker reinforces this focus of attention in order to maintain and increase his control. The victim may experience dissociation between thought and behavior. Behaviorally, the victim typically demonstrates a cooperative pseudo-calmness. Cognitively, the victim loses the ability to think rationally and emotionally he or she is in turmoil. Symonds (1980b) terms this second initial phase of captivity "traumatic psychological infantilism" (p. 40).

Following the initial shock of being taken captive, a number of identifiable, but sometimes different, emotional and behavioral clusters have been observed in victims, including the: (1) Stockholm Syndrome

(Hacker, 1976); (2) Common Sense Syndrome (Strentz, 1977); (3) Survi-
vor Identification Syndrome (Schlossberg, 1980); (4) Hostage Response
Syndrome (Wesselius & DeSarno, 1983); (5) Hostage Identification
Syndrome (Turner, 1985); (6) London Syndrome (Olin & Born, 1983);
and (7) "Hysterical-Whiner" Syndrome (Fuselier, 1991). The first five
of these enumerated syndromes refer to the paradoxical situation where
a victim may develop positive feelings for his or her hostage taker. This
is often associated with negative feelings directed toward authorities.
When a hostage taker does not harm the victim, the captive may feel a
sense of gratitude. Symonds (1980b) describes this as "pathological
bonding" (p. 41), and most crisis professionals utilize Hacker's (1976)
term–Stockholm Syndrome–when discussing this phenomenon.

Although once thought to be a common hostage experience, the
Stockholm Syndrome is believed by many crisis negotiators to be an in-
frequent occurrence and only under certain circumstances. Two conditions that may precipitate development of the Stockholm Syndrome are
time and positive contact between victim and perpetrator. However, the
positive contact must be initiated by the hostage taker (Lanceley, 1999).
If there has been no contact between the hostage taker and victim, or if
the hostage taker has abused the hostage, the Stockholm Syndrome will
not develop. Also, it is highly unlikely that a victim who has had a previous relationship with the perpetrator will develop the Stockholm Syndrome. Likewise, different cultural values, lack of a common language,
and preexisting racial, ethnic, religious, or ideological prejudices can
work to hinder the development of a positive bond between hostage
taker and victim. In these situations, the passage of time may actually
increase the risk of harm to the hostages, since the perpetrator's negative view of the victim is selectively reinforced (Turner, 1985).

The last two syndromes mentioned above refer to the situation where
a victim acts in a manner that provokes his or her death. The London
Syndrome was observed in 1981 during the Iranian Embassy siege in
London, England. During the siege, a hostage named Abbas Lavasani
continuously argued with the hostage takers even though his fellow
hostages urged him not to do so. After several days into the siege, the
hostage takers decided to kill a hostage and they chose Lavasani. The
same phenomenon occurred in June of 1986 in Beverly Hills, California. After a botched jewelry store holdup that turned into a hostage situation, the perpetrator killed a security guard who was tied and lying face
down on the floor. The hostage taker killed the guard because the victim
"was talking back to me" (Fuselier, 1991, p. 714).

The Hysterical-Whiner Syndrome represents the other extreme of the emotional response continuum. As opposed to the aggressiveness of the London Syndrome, a victim who draws attention to himself or herself by crying, whining, and/or being overly solicitous or overly compliant characterizes this latter syndrome. Such an incident occurred in Rochester, New York, in 1985 when an African-American male held a racially diverse group of white and African-American men and women hostage. The principle motive for the hostage taking was perceived to be racial discrimination. Nevertheless, when a deadline passed without his demands being met, the perpetrator selected a black woman to kill. He did so because he was irked by the victim's continual crying, whining, and pleading for mercy.

Rescued hostages require special care. Following rescue, a significant proportion of victims suffer diagnosable mental disorders secondary to their experience, principally post-traumatic stress disorder (Allondi, 1994; Vila, Porche, & Mouren-Simeoni, 1999; Wesselius & DeSarno, 1983). For example, Easton and Turner (1991) found that between 25% and 50% of the British subjects who were held hostage in Kuwait during the Persian Gulf War reported psychological problems nine to 10 months after their release. Likewise, two months after a school hostage incident in Paris, Vila, Porche, and Mouren-Simeoni (1999) observed diagnosable mental disorders in 72% of the children evaluated (26 out of 29 child hostages). More specifically, these researchers noted seven cases of PTSD, 11 cases of subclinical PTSD, three cases of separation anxiety, one case of phobia, and two cases of major depressive disorder.

Furthermore, it appears that the victims' psychological problems may last for quite some time. For example, Van der Ploeg and Kleijn (1989) noted that 32% of the 138 hostages they studied reported continuing psychological trauma nine years after a train hostage incident in The Netherlands. Terr (1991) observed that 100% of the 25 children hostages she studied reported continuing psychological problems four years after the Chowchilla school-bus kidnapping incident. Desivilya, Gal, and Ayalon (1996) found that even 17 years after a barricade hostage event at a school in Israel, a majority of the 76 survivors reported symptoms of traumatic stress (39% reported four symptoms; 52% reported five to eight symptoms; and 9% reported nine or more symptoms).

Certain factors appear to be correlated with increased risk of long-term psychological problems following victim rescue, including witnessing physical violence, suffering physical violence, and not receiving psychological debriefing after release (Bisson, Searle, & Srinivasan, 1998; Desivilya, Gal, & Ayalon, 1996; Vila, Porche, & Mouren-Simeoni, 1999).

McDuff (1992) stated that specially trained intervention teams need to work with released captives before they return to their everyday life. The goals of this intervention are to educate the victims and their families with respect to the psychological consequences of trauma, foster a supportive social network amongst the victims, and prevent others (particularly the media) from intruding upon the victims. Symonds (1983) noted that treatment for released hostages should revolve around reassurance that the victim's behavior during captivity was acceptable, restoration of feelings of power, reduction of feelings of isolation, diminishment of feelings of helplessness, and encouragement of feelings of control.

CONCLUSION

Over the past 30 years, a vast literature has developed regarding crisis negotiation; nevertheless, more work needs to be done. Four areas that are ripe for research are: (1) documentation and analysis of hostage/barricade events; (2) analysis and improvement of crisis negotiation techniques; (3) development and improvement of victim treatment techniques; and (4) exploring the impact of the media on the outcome of hostage/barricade events. It is particularly important to note that local hostage/barricade incident databases should be maintained, similar to the one kept at the Department of Psychiatry and Behavioral Sciences, University of Louisville School of Medicine (Feldmann, 1998). Careful documentation and analysis is crucial not only for individual negotiation success, but also for developing a better understanding of crisis events. Thus, it is recommended that negotiating teams make greater use of dedicated software programs, such as the Crisis Negotiator, during crisis incidents. The structured information generated by such software programs helps meet both the immediate goal of resolving the crisis incident as well as the long-term goal of providing a systematic record of the event for inclusion in regional databases. With the development and maintenance of regional databases, local hostage recovery programs will be better able to obtain relevant information regarding hostage/barricade incidents in their community and analyze their negotiation style and effectiveness.

REFERENCES

Allondi, F. A. (1994). Post-traumatic stress disorder in hostages and victims of torture. *Psychiatric Clinics of North America, 17,* 279-288.

American Psychiatric Association (1994). *Diagnostic and statistical manual of mental disorders (4th ed.).* Washington, DC: Author.

Bahn, C. & Louden, R. J. (1999). Hostage negotiation as a team enterprise. *Group, 23,* 77-85.

Bisson, J. I., Searle, M. M., & Srinivasan, M. (1998). Follow-up study of British military hostages and their families held in Kuwait during the gulf war. *British Journal of Medical Psychology, 71,* 247-252.

Bolz, F. & Hershey, E. (1979). *Hostage cop.* New York: Rawson, Wade.

Butler, W. M., Leitenberg, H., & Fuselier, G. D. (1993). The use of mental health professional consultants to police hostage negotiation teams. *Behavioral Sciences & the Law, 11,* 213-221.

Call, J. A. (1996). The hostage triad: Takers, victims, and negotiators. In H. V. Hall (Ed.), *Lethal violence 2000: A sourcebook on fatal domestic, acquaintance and stranger aggression* (pp. 561-588). Kamuela, HI: Pacific Institute for the Study of Conflict and Aggression.

Cooper, H. H. A. (1981). *The hostage takers.* Boulder, CO: Paladin Press.

Crisis Management Consultants, Inc. (2002). *Crisis negotiator 1.0 manual.* Oklahoma City, OK: Author.

Desivilya, H. S., Gal, R., & Ayalon, O. (1996). Extent of victimization, traumatic stress symptoms, and adjustment of terrorist assault survivors: A long term follow-up. *Journal of Traumatic Stress, 9,* 881-889.

Donohue, W. A., Ramesh, C., Kaufmann, G., & Smith, R. (1991). Crisis bargaining in intense conflict situations. *International Journal of Group Tensions, 21,* 133-153.

Donohue, W. A. & Roberto, A. J. (1993). Relational development as negotiated order in hostage negotiation. *Human Communication Research, 20,* 175-198.

Donohue, W. A. & Roberto, A. J. (1996). An empirical examination of three models of integrative and distributive bargaining. *International Journal of Conflict Management, 7,* 209-229.

Downs vs. United States, 522 R. 2d 990 (6th Cir. 1975).

Easton, J. A. & Turner, S. W. (1991). Detention of British citizens as hostages in the Gulf War: Health, psychological and family consequences. *British Medical Journal, 303,* 1231-1234.

Feldmann, T. B. (1998). *Characteristics of hostage and barricade incident: Implications for negotiation strategies and training.* Unpublished manuscript, Department of Psychiatry and Behavioral Sciences, University of Louisville School of Medicine, Louisville, KY.

Ferracuti, F. (1982). A sociopsychiatric interpretation of terrorism. *Annals of the American Academy of Political and Social Sciences, 463,* 129-140.

Friedland, N. & Merari, A. (1992). Hostage events: Descriptive profile and analysis of outcomes. *Journal of Applied Social Psychology, 22,* 134-156.

Fuselier, G. D. (1988). Hostage negotiation consultant: Emerging role for the clinical psychologist. *Professional Psychology: Research and Practice, 19,* 175-179.

Fuselier, G. D. (1991). Hostage negotiation: Issues and applications. In R. Gal & A. D. Mangelsdorff (Eds.), *Handbook of military psychology* (pp. 711-723). New York: John Wiley and Sons.

Fuselier, G. D. & Romana, S. (1996, October). *Behavioral aspects of hostage negotiation.* Symposium conducted at the University of Colorado Health Sciences Center, Denver, CO.

Fuselier, G. D. & Van Zandt, C. R. (1987). *A practical overview of hostage negotiations.* Unpublished manuscript, FBI Academy, Quantico, VA.

Fuselier, G. D., Van Zandt, C. R., & Lanceley, F. J. (1991). High risk factors and the "action criteria" in hostage/barricade situations. *FBI Law Enforcement Bulletin, 60(1),* 6-12.

Gist, R. G. & Perry, J. D. (1985). Perspectives on negotiation in local jurisdictions: Part I. A different typology of situations. *FBI Law Enforcement Bulletin, 54(11),* 21-24.

Hacker, F. J. (1976). *Crusaders, criminals, crazies: Terror and terrorism in our time.* New York: W. W. Norton.

Hatcher, G., Mohandie, K., Turner, J., & Gelles, M. G. (1998). The role of the psychologist in crisis/hostage negotiations. *Behavioral Sciences & the Law, 16,* 455-472.

Head, W. B. (1990). The hostage response: An examination of the U.S. law enforcement practices concerning hostage incidents. *Dissertation Abstracts International, 50,* 4111-A.

Higginbotham, J. (1994). Legal issues in crisis management. *FBI Law Enforcement Bulletin, 63(6),* 27-32.

Kennedy, H. G. & Dyer, D. E. (1992). Parental hostage takers. *British Journal of Psychiatry, 160,* 410-412.

Knutson, J. N. (1980). The dynamics of the hostage taker: Some major variants. *Annals of the New York Academy of Sciences, 347,* 117-128.

Lanceley, F. L. (1999). *On-scene guide for crisis negotiation.* Boca Raton, FL: CRC Press.

McDuff, D. R. (1992). Social issues in the management of released hostages. *Hospital and Community Psychiatry, 43,* 825-828.

Mickolus, E. (1976). Negotiating for hostages: A policy dilemma. *Orbis, 19,* 1309-1325.

Miron, M. & Goldstein, A. (1979). *Hostage.* New York: Pergamon Press.

Olin, W. R. & Born, D. G. (1983). A behavioral approach to hostage situations. *FBI Law Enforcement Bulletin, 52(1),* 19-24.

Pearce, K. I. (1977). Police negotiations: A new role for the community psychiatrist. *Canadian Psychiatric Association Journal, 22,* 171-175.

Rahe, R. H., Karson, S., Howard, N. S., Rubin, R. T., & Poland, R. E. (1990). Psychological and physiological assessments on American hostages freed from captivity in Iran. *Psychosomatic Medicine, 52,* 1-16.

Rogan, R. G., Donohue, W. A., & Lyles, J. (1990). Gaining and exercising control in hostage negotiations using empathic perspective-taking. *International Journal of Group Tensions, 20,* 77-91.

Schlossberg, H. (1980). Values and organization in hostage and crisis negotiation teams. *Annals of the New York Academy of Sciences, 347,* 113-116.

Soskis, D. A. & Van Zandt, C. R. (1986). Hostage negotiation: Law enforcement's most effective nonlethal weapon. *Behavioral Sciences & the Law, 4,* 423-435.

Strentz, T. (1977). *Survival adaptation . . . the common sense syndrome*. Unpublished manuscript, FBI Academy, Quantico, VA.

Strentz, T. (1980). The Stockholm Syndrome: Law enforcement policy and ego defenses of the hostage. *Annals of the New York Academy of Sciences, 347*, 137-150.

Strentz, T. (1986). Negotiating with the hostage-taker exhibiting paranoid-schizophrenic symptoms. *Journal of Police Science and Administration, 14*, 12-17.

Symonds, M. (1980a). Victims' responses to terror. *Annals of the New York Academy of Sciences, 347*, 129-136.

Symonds, M. (1980b). Acute responses of victims to terror. *Evaluation and Change [Special Issue]*, 39-41.

Symonds, M. (1983). Victimization and rehabilitative treatment. In B. Eichelman, D. Soskis, & W. Reid (Eds.), *Terrorism: Interdisciplinary perspectives* (pp. 69-81). Washington, DC: American Psychiatric Association.

Terr, L. C. (1983). Chowchilla revisited: The effects of psychic trauma four years after a school-bus kidnapping. *American Journal of Psychiatry, 140*, 1543-1550.

Turner, J. T. (1985). Factors influencing the development of the hostage identification syndrome. *Political Psychology, 6*, 705-711.

Van der Ploeg, H. K. & Kleijn, W. C. (1989). Being held hostage in the Netherlands: A study of long-term after effects. *Journal of Traumatic Stress, 2*, 153-169.

Vila, G., Porche, L-M., & Mouren-Simeoni, M-C. (1999). An 18-month longitudinal study of posttraumatic disorders in children who were taken hostage in their school. *Psychosomatic Medicine, 61*, 746-766.

Wesselius, C. L. & DeSarno, J. V. (1983). The anatomy of a hostage situation. *Behavioral Sciences & the Law, 1*, 33-45.

Ethical Concerns in Forensic Consultation Regarding National Safety and Security

Charles Patrick Ewing
Michael G. Gelles

SUMMARY. Psychologists and psychiatrists are frequently called upon to provide consultation in terrorism, espionage and/or intelligence cases involving the vital interests of the United States. Often these are cases in which the client is not the individual about whom advice is being sought but rather the military, a government intelligence agency, or law enforcement, and the consultant must act within parameters set by law and/or dictated by concerns for public safety or national security. In some of these cases, psychological and psychiatric consultants are asked to function in non-traditional roles that may conflict with the currently accepted ethical principles of their professions. This article explores some of the ethical dilemmas peculiar to consultations in this increasingly important context. *[Article copies available for a fee from The Haworth Document Delivery Service: 1-800-HAWORTH. E-mail address: <docdelivery@ haworthpress.com> Website: <http://www.HaworthPress.com> © 2003 by The Haworth Press, Inc. All rights reserved.]*

Charles Patrick Ewing, JD, PhD, ABPP (Forensic Psychology), is Professor of Law at the State University of New York.

Michael G. Gelles, PsyD, is Chief Psychologist of the United States Naval Criminal Investigation Service.

Address correspondence to: Charles Patrick Ewing, University at Buffalo School of Law, Buffalo, NY 14260 (E-mail: cewing@buffalo.edu).

[Haworth co-indexing entry note]: "Ethical Concerns in Forensic Consultation Regarding National Safety and Security." Ewing, Charles Patrick, and Michael G. Gelles. Co-published simultaneously in *Journal of Threat Assessment* (The Haworth Press, Inc.) Vol. 2, No. 3, 2003, pp. 95-107; and: *Terrorism: Strategies for Intervention* (ed: Harold V. Hall) The Haworth Press, Inc., 2003, pp. 95-107. Single or multiple copies of this article are available for a fee from The Haworth Document Delivery Service [1-800-HAWORTH, 9:00 a.m. - 5:00 p.m. (EST). E-mail address: docdelivery@haworthpress.com].

KEYWORDS. Ethics, terrorism, espionage, intelligence, consultation, national security

For many years, psychologists and psychiatrists have consulted on cases in which the client is either a military, national security or law enforcement agency. In many such consultations, these forensic professionals have been asked to render opinions regarding third parties known or suspected to pose a threat to national safety and security. Since the terrorist attacks of September 11, 2001, demand for such consultations has increased, as have both the stakes and expectations for these consultations. Psychologists and psychiatrists are now being asked to provide consultation in terrorism, intelligence and espionage cases where the well-being and lives of hundreds, thousands, perhaps even millions of people hang in the balance. Moreover, they are being asked to function in non-traditional roles that, while serving the critical interests of the United States, may in some instances conflict with the standard ethical principles of psychology and psychiatry.

In providing consultation to military, national security and law enforcement agencies, forensic mental health professionals sometimes never meet the individual about whom consultation is sought. In other instances, these professionals not only meet but evaluate the individual in question. In either event, however, there is no traditional "doctor-patient" relationship, and the "client" is not the individual assessed but the governmental entity or agency seeking the consultation.

While all psychologists and psychiatrists must adhere to well-established ethical and practice standards, most of these principles contemplate traditional clinical situations in which the professional is presumed to be acting in the best interest of the individual being assessed and has direct or at least shared responsibility for case management. When serving as consultants to the military, an intelligence agency or law enforcement, however, psychologists and psychiatrists generally are not functioning in a traditional clinical role, do not have ultimate authority and responsibility for case management, and are not acting in the best interest of the individual being assessed. Indeed, in many instances, the professional acts with the knowledge that his or her input will likely have negative consequences for the individual in question (e.g., arrest, detention, prosecution, physical injury or even death).

To date, the ethical principles and standards of practice pertaining to this growing area of forensic consultation have received little formal discussion. As a result, many psychologists and psychiatrists who work with military, intelligence, and law enforcement agencies now find themselves in uncharted ethical waters. As a further result, some of these professionals may steer clear of such vital work for fear of stepping on an ethical land-mine and jeopardizing their professional standing, licenses, and livelihoods.

This article briefly explores some of the ethical concerns peculiar to psychological and psychiatric consultation where the client is not the individual about whom advice is being sought but rather the military, government intelligence, or law enforcement, and the consultant must act within parameters set by law and/or dictated by concerns for public safety or national security.

Among the issues to be considered are ethical concerns that arise in the following contexts:

1. The consultant's input may have serious consequences for the individual in question but, for legal and/or public safety/national security reasons, the consultant has no direct access to the individual.
2. The consultant has professional contact with the individual in question but law, national security and/or public safety concerns dictate that the true purpose of the contact be withheld from the subject of the investigation.
3. Certain aspects of the consultant's role are dictated in part by legal parameters outside the consultant's control.

PERTINENT STATEMENTS OF ETHICAL PRINCIPLES

The professional practices of psychologists and psychiatrists are directed not only by individual conscience but also by written guidelines. For psychologists, these guidelines take the form of the American Psychological Association's "Ethical Principles of Psychologists" (American Psychological Association, 1992; hereinafter "APA Ethical Principles") and the "Specialty Guidelines for Forensic Psychologists" jointly promulgated by the American Psychology-Law Society and the American Academy of Forensic Psychology (Committee on Ethical Guidelines for Forensic Psychologists, 1991; hereinafter "APLS-AAFP Specialty Guidelines"). For psychiatrists, such guidelines are spelled out in the American Psychiatric Association's "Principles of Medical Ethics with Annotations Especially Applicable to Psychiatry" (American Psychiatric Association, 1998; hereinafter "Principles of Medical Ethics") and the "Ethical Guidelines for the Practice of Forensic Psychiatry" developed by the American Academy of Psychiatry and the Law (American Academy of Psychiatry & the Law, 1995; hereinafter "AAPL Ethical Guidelines").

None of these statements of ethical principles are legally binding. Indeed, they have no directly enforceable effect on anyone but members of the specific organizations that developed them. Still, these various guidelines are widely recognized and accepted by many if not most psychologists and psychiatrists, particularly those who practice in forensic specialties. Moreover, in many jurisdictions, professionals who violate these principles risk not only sanction by the relevant professional organization but also professional discipline by their state licensing boards. Thus, in offering a practical examination of the ethical dilemmas that arise in the above-noted contexts, these four sets of standards provide both a natural and essential starting point.

CONSULTANT HAS NO CONTACT WITH THE SUBJECT AND CONSULTATION MAY LEAD TO ADVERSE LEGAL CONSEQUENCES FOR THE SUBJECT

Military, national security, and law enforcement operations often require psychological assessments of subjects who are suspected of espionage, conspiracy, terrorism, treason or other crimes against the national safety and security. Typically such assessments are conducted indirectly. There is no contact between the subject and the psychologist or psychiatrist. Instead, the authorities gather pertinent information regarding the suspect and present those data to the mental health consultant for analysis and opinion.

While such assessments are now done frequently, for obvious national security reasons they are done covertly and their techniques and findings are sensitive and for official use only, if not classified. One recent case, however, can now be discussed in detail because its facts have become a matter of public record. Suspected of spying, Theresa Squillacote, a U.S. Defense Department lawyer, and her husband, Kurt Stand, were the subject of a secret court order obtained by federal agents. Under the order, the couple was placed under round-the-clock surveillance, their phones were tapped, their home secretly bugged and searched, and their computer files surreptitiously downloaded. Information gathered by federal agents, including intercepted conversations with Squillacote's psychotherapist, were used to create a psychological profile of Squillacote. The profile, developed by the FBI's Behavioral

Analysis Program (BAP), which included a psychologist, was designed "to examine [Squillacote's] personality . . . and based on this examination, to provide suggestions . . . that could be used in furthering the objective of this investigation to obtain evidence regarding the subject's espionage activity" (*United States v. Squillacote*, 2001, p. 550).

The BAP profile concluded that Squillacote suffered from depression, was taking anti-depressant medications, had a "narcissistic" and "histrionic" personality, and demonstrated "poor impulse control," "excessively emotional behavior," and an excessive need for "reassurance, approval, and praise" (Petition for a Writ of Certiorari, *United States v. Squillacote*, 2000).

The profilers offered specific recommendations on how to exploit Squillacote's "emotional vulnerability" (*United States v. Squillacote*, p. 550). The BAP report suggested using a sting operation conducted by a mature male undercover agent, who should "capitalize on [Squillacote's] fantasies and intrigue" by making a "friendly overture," and "acting professional and somewhat aloof yet responsive to her moods" (*Squillacote*, p. 551). According to the recommendation, "The initial meeting should be brief and leave Squillacote beguiled and craving more attention" (*Squillacote*, p. 551).

The recommended operation was implemented and was effective. Squillacote met four times with an undercover FBI agent posing as a South African intelligence official, and provided him with classified documents she obtained from the Department of Defense. After several months of contacts with the agent, Squillacote was arrested and convicted of conspiracy to transmit information relating to the national defense, attempted transmission of national defense information, obtaining national defense information, and making false statements.

Some commentators found the work of the FBI psychologist in the Squillacote case to be unethical. For example, a forensic psychiatrist, Janofsky (2001), argued that for a psychiatrist to have engaged in such professional conduct would have constituted "a gross violation of professional ethics, because the overt intent of the BAP was to deceive deliberately and exploit the defendant in ways directly related to her unique psychological vulnerabilities" (p. 450).

Another psychiatrist, Candilis (2001), concluded that "Professional ethics, the social contract, and the common balance between individual and state's rights begin to militate against the kind of analysis conducted by the FBI's psychologist" (pp. 454-455). Candilis also urged that such conduct gave the appearance of wrongdoing and that creating such appearance is unethical because it damages trust in the professions. In her words, "The mere perception of a government psychologist's disavowing forensic protections and using deception against a suicidal individual is damaging . . . Even if overstated, the scenario's emotional valence undermines both psychology and governance" (p. 455).

On the other hand, others saw no such ethical violations here. For example, an FBI Special Agent, Schafer (2001), dismissed Janofsky's ethical concerns as simply one man's opinion: "If the actions of a person do not violate the law or the professional ethics of the group to which the individual belongs, then the person's actions become a matter of personal choices and opinions. Thus, Janofsky's charge that the FBI's BAP psychologist violated the code of professional ethics should read: 'Based on my opinion, the actions of the FBI's BAP psychologist do not comport with the personal expectations I have as to how I believe a professional psychologist should act' " (p. 446).

Grisso (2001) observed that "psychologists and psychiatrists often must do harm" and doing such harm is not necessarily unethical. As Grisso noted, doing such harm is potentially justified "when weighed against the social consequences if one failed to risk the chances of that harm." As Grisso put it, "How a professional weighs the competing positive values in a case such as this depends in part on the professional's own values. One professional places more weight on the sanctity of the individual and the damage to the public's perception of 'mental health' professionals whose ethics would allow them to exploit the weaknesses of persons with mental illnesses. Another appeals to the greater good to society when psychology is applied to protect the national interest from political subversion" (pp. 459-460).

Both Schafer and Grisso appear to be correct. Not only is the conduct of the psychologist in this case not specifically proscribed by any of the pertinent statements of ethical principles, but the propriety of such conduct is implicitly endorsed by these statements and justified by the kind of balancing test Grisso implicitly suggests.

Both the "Principles of Medical Ethics" and the "APA Ethical Principles" make it clear that psychologists and psychiatrists are responsible not only to individuals but to society at large. The "Principles of Medical Ethics" state that "a physician must recognize responsibility not only to patients, but also to society . . ." (Preamble) and that "psychiatrists are encouraged to serve society by advising and consulting with the executive, legislative and judiciary branches of the government" (Section 7.1).

The "APA Ethical Principles" state that "Psychologists seek to contribute to the welfare of those with whom they interact professionally. In their professional actions, psychologists weigh the welfare and rights of their patients or clients, students, supervisees, human research participants, and other affected persons, and the welfare of animal subjects of research. When conflicts occur among psychologists' obligations or concerns, they attempt to resolve these conflicts and to perform their roles in a responsible fashion that avoids or minimizes harm" (Principle E).

The APA Ethical Principles also indicate that "Psychologists are aware of their professional and scientific responsibilities to the community and the society in which they work and live. They apply and make public their knowledge of psychology in order to contribute to human welfare. Psychologists are concerned about and work to mitigate the causes of human suffering" (Principle F).

These global statements of ethical principles support the notion advanced by Grisso that the consequences of doing harm to an individual, as in the Squillacote matter, must be balanced against the consequences of not doing such harm. While one can only speculate what the harm to the United States and its citizens might have been had Squillacote not been apprehended, it is not unreasonable to suggest that such harm might have been substantial. Many instances of espionage have not only undermined national safety and security but have resulted in many deaths. The FBI psychologist did not violate the ethical principles of his profession but rather upheld those principles by risking harm to one individual in order to avert a potentially much greater harm to a multitude of individuals.

CONSULTANT HAS CONTACT WITH THE SUBJECT BUT THE SUBJECT IS NOT AWARE OF THE CONSULTANT'S FUNCTION

In some instances, unlike the Squillacote investigation, mental health consultants to military, national security, and law enforcement operations have direct access to subjects they are asked to evaluate. If the subject of the evaluation is fully informed of the identity and profession of the evaluator and the nature and potential consequences of the evaluation, and gives informed consent to the evaluation, there will usually be no ethical concern. However, in many cases, for strategic reasons, authorities may wish to have a subject covertly evaluated by a mental health professional or overtly evaluated but without revealing the true nature of the evaluation to the subject. Consider several cases of this sort:

In the first, the government has identified a volunteer source who is providing agents with valuable information regarding a possible leak of classified and highly sensitive information. The leak, if not stopped, could lead to the deaths of numerous government intelligence agents abroad. This individual realizes that his assignment is dangerous and could result in his being seriously harmed, even killed. Government agents have asked a mental health professional to meet with this individual to help him manage his anxiety. The individual is aware of this aspect of the professional's function but is not aware that agents have also asked the professional to assess his motivation, emotional stability, social skills and intellect so as to best utilize his abilities and to maintain his safety and continued cooperation.

In a second case, a soldier, the subject of an espionage investigation, is suspected of passing to foreign agents classified data that could impact the lives of hundreds of soldiers and sailors currently deployed in a combat zone. At the behest of investigators, the suspect is led by superior officers to believe that he is being considered for reassignment to a more desirable position. The suspect is also asked to undergo a psychological evaluation purportedly related to the possible new assignment but actually designed to assess the suspect's personality and behavior so as to develop useful interview and interrogation strategies. The results of the evaluation are later used by investigators to facilitate interrogation that leads to a confession.

In a third case, a psychologist is asked to attend a cocktail party where one of the numerous guests will be the suspect in an ongoing espionage investigation. The psychologist is directed to mingle, observe the suspect and, if possible, engage the suspect in conversation in order to conduct a brief assessment for purposes of helping to develop an arrest and interrogation plan. The psychologist attends the party, observes and converses with the suspect, and passes his observations and opinions to the investigators, who use them to develop a plan to detain and question the suspect.

In the fourth case, a psychologist is asked to consult with military and intelligence officials who are interrogating detainees suspected of participation in past terrorist acts, conspiracy to commit further acts of terrorism, and knowledge of others who have committed such acts against the United States. The purpose of the interrogation is to gather evidence that may lead to criminal charges against (or exoneration of) the detainees and others but also may be used to prevent future acts of terrorism.

In some of these investigations, the psychologist consultant either participates in or observes the interview but the detainee is not informed of the professional identity of the psychologist. In any event, the psychologist utilizes his or her psychological training and experience to assist the government in gaining the detainee's cooperation and/or obtaining behavioral data that will otherwise materially assist the interrogators.

In all of the above situations, the balancing test discussed earlier would appear to ethically justify the conduct of the mental health professional. Clearly in each of these cases, the harm imposed (active or passive deception by the professional leading to potentially adverse consequences for the subject) is arguably much less than the harm likely to be avoided (continued espionage and/or terrorism that could cost many lives and seriously undermine national security). However, the mental health professional's conduct in each of these cases just as clearly violates specific aspects of the pertinent statements of ethical principles.

The "Principles of Medical Ethics" indicate that "Psychiatrists are often asked to examine individuals for security purposes, to determine suitability for various jobs, and to determine legal competence. The psychiatrist must fully describe the nature and purpose and lack of confidentiality of the examination to the examinee at the beginning of the examination" (Section 4.6). This basic restatement of the fundamental requirement of informed consent is echoed in the "APA Ethical Principles" which state that: "When a psychologist agrees to provide services to a person or entity at the request of a third party, the psychologist clarifies to the extent feasible, at the outset of the service, the nature of the relationship with each party. This clarification includes the role of the psychologist (such as therapist, organizational consultant, diagnostician, or expert witness), the probable uses of the services provided or the information obtained, and the fact that there may be limits to confidentiality . . . If there is a foreseeable risk of the psychologist's being called upon to perform conflicting roles because of the involvement of a third party, the psychologist clarifies the nature and direction of his or her responsibilities, keeps all parties appropriately informed as matters develop . . . " (Section 1.21(a)).

Similarly, the "AAPL Ethical Guidelines" state that "The informed consent of the subject of a forensic evaluation is obtained when possible. Where consent is not required, notice is given to the evaluee of the nature of the evaluation. If the evaluee is not competent to give consent, substituted consent is obtained in hereinafter accordance with the laws of the jurisdiction" (Section III).

The "APLS-AAFP Specialty Guidelines" are even more explicit, specifying that "Forensic psychologists have an obligation to ensure that prospective clients are informed of their legal rights with respect to the anticipated forensic service, of the purposes of any evaluation, of the nature of procedures to be employed, of the intended uses of any product of their services, and of the party who has employed the forensic psychologist" (p. 659).

ASPECTS OF THE CONSULTANT'S INVOLVEMENT ARE DICTATED BY LEGAL PARAMETERS OUTSIDE THE CONSULTANT'S CONTROL

Finally, in some cases, certain aspects of the mental health consultant's involvement in national security cases are dictated by legal concerns outside the consultant's control. Consider, for example, a case in which a government psychologist interacts with an espionage suspect agents believe has passed classified information to foreign enemies, thereby potentially endangering the lives of hundreds of military personnel. During interrogation, the subject claims not to be able to recall what, if anything, he has done in that regard and suggests that perhaps a mental health expert could help restore his recollection. The agents arrange to have the suspect interviewed by a government psychologist who makes clear his professional identity, the purpose of the interview as he understands it, his role in the matter, his employment by the government, and his affiliation with federal agents who have been interrogating the suspect. The suspect is not promised confidentiality; indeed, he is specifically given the standard Miranda warnings with regard to the use of any incriminating statements. The suspect gives informed consent to be interviewed by the psychologist in the presence of the federal agents who have been interrogating him. However, pursuant to legal requirements but unknown to the suspect, the interview is videotaped for the protection of the subject, the psychologist, and the agents, as well as to preserve any evidence that might emerge from the interview.

Has the psychologist acted unethically by conducting the interview without informing the suspect of the videotaping? Once again, given the nature of the case (espionage) and the stakes involved (possible death for hundreds of American military personnel), the simple balancing test would appear to justify the implicit deception involved in not informing the suspect that the interview is being videotaped. But also again, just as clearly, if held to the formal ethical standards of the mental health professions, the psychologist's conduct might well be judged a violation of the informed consent doctrine spelled out in the "Principles of Medical Ethics," the "APA Ethical Principles," the "AAPL Ethical Guidelines" and the "APLS-AAFP Specialty Guidelines" described in the preceding section of this article. Moreover, even though videotaping the interview without the subject's knowledge was done pursuant to legal requirements, the psychologist might still be regarded as violating ethical standards. For example, the APA Ethical Principles state that: "In the process of making decisions regarding their professional behavior, psychologists must consider this Ethics Code, in addition to applicable laws and psychology board regulations. If the Ethics Code establishes a higher standard of conduct than is required by law, psychologists must meet the higher ethical standard" (Introduction).

SUMMARY AND A CALL TO ACTION

As the above examples illustrate, strict application of the prevailing ethical standards in psychology and psychiatry would effectively preclude psychologists and psychiatrists from engaging in most of the kinds of professional conduct described in this article. Indeed, in the eyes of some, psychologists and psychiatrists should be ethically precluded from engaging in any of the conduct described.

Such judgments, if taken seriously, put many government psychologists and psychiatrists between the proverbial rock and hard place. Their employment duties, allegiance to their nation, respect for human life and common sense all militate in favor of the kind of professional conduct described in this article–i.e., professional practice utilizing psychological and psychiatric expertise to reduce threats to our national safety and security. But as things stand now, by engaging in such conduct, they risk disrespecting the ethical principles of their professions, censure by or expulsion from their professional organizations, and possible suspension or loss of their professional licenses to practice.

Imposing the sort of balancing test discussed earlier would, in our view, render the professional conduct described in this article ethical. At the same time, however, such a standard might also place the stamp of professional ethical approval on conduct that we and others would regard as clearly unethical–e.g., consultation regarding the use of psychological torture of a terrorist suspect in order to obtain information that would save the lives of thousands of potential victims. Moreover, we acknowledge that not all psychologists and psychiatrists would agree with our analysis. Thus, even in these relatively ordinary national security cases, the ultimate ethical judgment would rest in large measure on how the balance happened to be struck and by whom. While some colleagues might join us in placing greater value on the protection of national safety and security, others such as Janofsky (2001) and Candilis (2001) might see a greater good served by eschewing deception and exploitation of individuals and avoiding what they see as the damage to public trust in the mental health professions engendered by such deception and exploitation.

Given the grave dangers faced by the United States and its allies post September 11, the government can ill afford to lose the input of psychologists, psychiatrists and other mental health professionals in cases involving national safety and security. Such input has been and will continue to be vital to protecting the lives of many Americans, civilian and military, at home and abroad. In order to maintain the ability and willingness of these dedicated professionals to continue in these roles, we cannot continue to place them in situations where the ethics of their conduct will be judged, *post hoc*, either by rules that have little if any relevance to their vital governmental functions or by professional organizations or licensing authorities based upon the weight the members of these bodies choose to afford competing interests.

There are not likely to be any simple solutions to this problem, and we suggest none. However, we believe that there is a compelling and immediate need not only for a dialogue regarding the competing interests that arise when psychologists and psychiatrists consult in national safety and security cases, but also for the development of realistic ethical standards appropriately tailored to specific practices of these professionals.

REFERENCES

American Academy of Law and Psychiatry (1995). Ethical guidelines for the practice of forensic psychiatry. Available at http://www.emory.edu/AAPL/ethics.htm; last visited October 17, 2002.

American Psychiatric Association (1981). Principles of medical ethics with annotations especially applicable to Psychiatry. Available at http://www.psych.org/apa_members/ethics_princpl.cfm; last visited October 17, 2002.

American Psychological Association (1992). Ethical principles of psychologists and code of conduct. Available at http://www.psychpage.com/ethics/ethicalprinciples.html; last visited October 17, 2002.

Candilis, P. J. (2001). Reply to Schafer: Ethics and state extremism in defense of liberty. *Journal of the American Academy of Psychiatry and the Law, 29,* 452-456.

Committee on Ethical Guidelines for Forensic Psychologists (1991). Specialty guidelines for forensic psychologists. *Law and Human Behavior, 15,* 655-665.

Grisso, T. (2001). Reply to Schafer: Doing harm ethically. *Journal of the American Academy of Psychiatry and the Law, 29,* 457-460.

Janofsky, J. S. (2001). Reply to Schafer: Exploitation of criminal suspects by mental health professionals is unethical. *Journal of the American Academy of Psychiatry and the Law, 29,* 449- 451.

Petition for a Writ of Certiorari, *United States v. Squillacote* (2000). Available at http://www.fas.org/irp/ops/ci/squill/petition.html; last visited October 17, 2002.

Schafer, J. R. (2001). The ethical use of psychology in criminal investigations. *Journal of the American Academy of Psychiatry and the Law, 29,* 445-446.

United States v. Squillacote, 221 F.3d 542 (2001).

Index

Active listening, 85,86
Agencies as clients, 96-97
Airliner hijacking, 71,80-81
Al-Queda, 59-60
American Academy of Forensic
    Psychology ethical guidelines,
    97-98,105
American Academy of Psychiatry and
    the Law ethical guidelines,
    98,103-104,105
American Psychiatric Association
    Principles of Medical Ethics,
    97-98,100-101,103,105
American Psychological Association
    ethical guidelines,
    97-98,100-101,103
American Psychology-Law Society
    ethical guidelines,
    97-98,103-104,105
American Type Culture Collection
    incident, 55
Anthrax
    evidence concealment, 57
    mailing incident, 41,52
    Soviet use, 44
    Sverdlosk outbreak, 44,46
Aum Shinrikyo Tokyo subway attacks,
    42,43

Bargaining for demands, 54
Barricade incidents, 69-95. *See also*
    Crisis negotiation
Behavioral analysis, 50-51. *See also*
    Lethal Violence Sequence
Behavioral development, of terrorists, 21
Biological adaptation theory, 10-11

Biological thought patterns, 15
Biological weapons, 41-68. *See also*
    Chemical/biological violence;
    Lethal Violence Sequence
Branch Davidians/Waco, Texas incident,
    78-79
Brigham Young University, 9-40

Chemical/biological violence, 6-7,41-68.
    See also Lethal Violence
    Sequence
    anthrax mailing incident, 44,52
    contextual features, 53
    Dark Winter exercise, 43
    descriptive statistics, 44,45
    existing prediction models, 44-50
    intervention recommendations, 62-65
    prediction by capability analysis, 46
    prediction by profiling, 48-50
    prediction by stages of conflict, 47-48
    prediction by weapon characteristics,
        46
    public indifference to threat, 52-53
    rational model of conflict, 47-48
    Tokyo subway attack, 42, 43
    Wasco County, Oregon attacks, 24
    White supremacist cyanide plot, 52
Children
    as hostages, 77
    Post-traumatic Stress Disorder in, 90
Client, agencies as, 96-97
Common Sense Syndrome, 89